ch

jv

THE JIM CROW LAWS
AND RACISM IN
AMERICAN HISTORY

Other titles *in American History*

THE JIM CROW LAWS AND RACISM IN AMERICAN HISTORY

David K. Fremon

Enslow Publishers, Inc.

40 Industrial Road   PO Box 38
Box 398   Aldershot
Berkeley Heights, NJ 07922 Hants GU12 6BP
USA   UK

http://www.enslow.com

Dedicated to Sonja, my true love

Library of Congress Cataloging-in-Publication Data

Fremon, David K.
    The Jim Crow laws and racism in American history / David K. Fremon.
        p. cm. — (In American history)
    Includes bibliographical references and index.
    Summary: Traces the struggles of African Americans from the end of
slavery through the period of Jim Crow segregation in the South, to the
civil rights movement and legal equality.
    ISBN 0-7660-1297-2
    1. Afro-Americans—Civil rights—Southern States—History—19th
century—Juvenile literature. 2. Afro-Americans—Segregation—Southern
States—History—19th century—Juvenile literature. 3. Afro-Americans—
Legal status, laws, etc.—Southern states—History. 4. Southern States—
Race relations—Juvenile literature. 5. Racism—Southern States—
History—Juvenile literature. 6. Afro-Americans—History—1863–1877—
Juvenile literature. 7. Afro-Americans—History—1877–1964—Juvenile
literature. [1. Afro-Americans—History—1863–1877. 2. Afro-
Americans—History—1877–1964. 3. Afro-Americans—Civil rights.
4. Race relations.] I. Title. II. Series.
E185.92 .F74 2000
305.896'073074—dc21

                                    99-041655

Printed in the United States of America

10 9 8 7 6 5 4 3 2 1

To Our Readers: All Internet addresses in this book were active and appropriate
at the time we went to press. Any comments or suggestions can be sent by e-mail
to Comments@enslow.com or to the address on the back cover.

Illustration Credits: Alabama Department of Archives and History,
p. 105; Enslow Publishers, Inc., p. 67; Library of Congress, pp. 19, 23,
34, 38, 43, 57, 60, 84, 87, 96, 110, 114; National Archives, pp. 9, 14,
108; Reproduced from the *Dictionary of American Portraits*, Published by
Dover Publications, Inc., in 1967, pp. 47, 50.

Cover Illustration: Library of Congress; National Archives.

★ CONTENTS ★

"THE MOST IMPORTANT DECISION"

Hundreds of people streamed into the United States Supreme Court building on May 17, 1954. Some of them saw the words "Equal Justice Under Law" carved in marble on the front of the building. That day, they would learn if those words held true.

The United States Supreme Court seldom announced in advance what cases it would decide. The Court gave its decision on cases on Mondays when it was in session. One Supreme Court case aroused more attention than all the others: *Brown* v. *Board of Education of Topeka, Kansas*.

Linda Brown, an eight-year-old African-American girl in Topeka, Kansas, wanted to go to a nearby public school. Topeka's board of education, which segregated (separated) students by race, refused the request. It claimed that Linda received an education equal to that of white students, even if she did not attend school with them. Brown's parents sued the district. This case would affect the entire nation. The issue was simple: Would black students be allowed to attend public schools with whites?

The Court, as usual, started at noon. After an hour of routine business, Chief Justice Earl Warren spoke the words everyone was waiting for. He declared, "I have for announcement the judgment and opinion of the Court in Number One *Brown et al.* versus *Board of Education of Topeka et al.*"[1]

Thurgood Marshall, hopeful but not certain, watched the justices. Marshall, a "shrewd, folksy black lawyer," had been an attorney for the National Association for the Advancement of Colored People (NAACP) since 1936.[2] He had argued more than fifty cases before the Supreme Court, winning most of them. He led the legal team that represented the Brown family, the plaintiffs in the case.

John W. Davis represented the Topeka Board of Education. The seventy-nine-year-old attorney, who had been the Democratic presidential nominee in 1924, was no stranger to the highest court. This was his one hundred fortieth appearance before the Supreme Court. It would be his most famous case.

Chief Justice Earl Warren read the Court's decision. He began by describing the background of the case. He mentioned the Fourteenth Amendment to the Constitution, which guaranteed equal rights to all citizens. He discussed the Supreme Court's 1896 *Plessy* v. *Ferguson* decision, which permitted "separate but equal" facilities for whites and blacks. He mentioned previous court cases regarding educational facilities.

Warren noted that, unlike many school systems in the South, Topeka had schools that appeared to be of

Thurgood Marshall (center) was the young lawyer who argued for the plaintiffs in the most famous civil rights case in history, Brown v. Board of Education.

equal quality for both races. "We must look instead to the effect of segregation itself on public education," he said. Then he asked the critical question: "Does segregation of children in public schools solely on the basis of race, even though the physical facilities and other 'tangible' factors be equal, deprive the children of the minority group of equal educational opportunities?"[3]

The gallery listened intently as Warren answered, "We believe it does." He added, "To separate them from others of similar age and qualifications solely because of their race generates a feeling of inferiority as to their status in the community that may affect their hearts and minds in a way unlikely ever to be undone."[4] Warren concluded, "In the field of public education, the doctrine of 'separate but equal' has no place. Separate educational facilities are inherently unequal."[5]

"If it was not the most important decision in the history of the Court, it was very close," commented Justice Stanley Reed.[6] For African-American children and adults, it marked a point of liberation. For years, Jim Crow, or segregation, laws had discriminated against blacks. The Court's decision would help lead to the laws' downfall.

The ruling met great opposition, especially in the South. Governor James Byrnes of South Carolina said he was "shocked" by the decision.[7] The Southern states would eventually pass more than four hundred fifty laws to try to prevent schools from carrying out the Court's decision.

IN EACH OF [THESE] CASES, MINORS OF THE NEGRO RACE, THROUGH THEIR LEGAL REPRESENTATIVES, SEEK THE AID OF THE COURTS IN OBTAINING ADMISSION TO THE PUBLIC SCHOOLS OF THEIR COMMUNITY ON A NONSEGREGATED BASIS. IN EACH INSTANCE, THEY HAD BEEN DENIED ADMISSION TO SCHOOLS ATTENDED BY WHITE CHILDREN UNDER LAWS REQUIRING OR PERMITTING SEGREGATION ACCORDING TO RACE. . . .

TODAY, EDUCATION IS PERHAPS THE MOST IMPORTANT FUNCTION OF STATE AND LOCAL GOVERNMENTS. . . . [I]T IS DOUBTFUL THAT ANY CHILD MAY REASONABLY BE EXPECTED TO SUCCEED IN LIFE IF HE IS DENIED THE OPPORTUNITY OF AN EDUCATION. SUCH AN OPPORTUNITY, WHERE THE STATE HAS UNDERTAKEN TO PROVIDE IT, IS A RIGHT WHICH MUST BE MADE AVAILABLE TO ALL ON EQUAL TERMS. . . .

WE CONCLUDE IN THE FIELD OF PUBLIC EDUCATION THE DOCTRINE OF "SEPARATE BUT EQUAL" HAS NO PLACE. SEPARATE EDUCATIONAL FACILITIES ARE INHERENTLY UNEQUAL.[8]

The Supreme Court's ruling in Brown *v.* Board of Education *in 1954 would set off the civil rights movement, which would forever change race relations in the United States.*

Other people saw the *Brown* decision differently. An African-American marine, upon hearing the verdict, said,

> My inner emotions must have been approximate to the Negro slaves' when they first heard about the Emancipation Proclamation [Abraham Lincoln's 1863 statement that would free the slaves in the South during the Civil War]. . . . On this momentous night of May 17, 1954 . . . I experienced a loyalty that I had never felt before. I was sure that this was the beginning of a new era in American democracy.[9]

The Supreme Court's decision would change the lives of millions, as it began to destroy the system of Jim Crow segregation that had existed almost since the end of the Civil War.

On April 9, 1865, Southern General Robert E. Lee signed a treaty with Union General Ulysses S. Grant that would lead to the end of the American Civil War. The Confederate states would have to recognize Union President Abraham Lincoln's Emancipation Proclamation of 1863. The South's slaves would soon be legally free.

LESS-THAN-FREE FREEDMEN

Black Codes and Northern Reactions

Freedom did not arrive at the same time and in the same way for all black Southerners. In large cities such as Richmond, Virginia, the word came instantly. Some white plantation owners, however, did not notify their former slaves of their freedom until months after the war's end.

At first, some freedmen (newly freed men and women) were led to believe that they could take over land on their former masters' plantations. But President Andrew Johnson dashed such hopes. His May 29, 1865, Proclamation of Amnesty pardoned most former Confederate soldiers. The law allowed

President Andrew Johnson, who took office after Abraham Lincoln was assassinated, disappointed many African Americans and their supporters with his leniency toward former Confederates after the Civil War.

them to take back any lands that might be occupied by African Americans.

Landless and poor, most without skills or jobs, former slaves could leave their plantations, but where would they go? Some set out to reunite with family members who had been sold by their former masters. Others went in search of better opportunities. This mobility disrupted life on the plantations. Former slave owners were used to having a stable, undemanding workforce. Emancipation changed the rules of life.

Some Southern whites were not upset about the slaves' emancipation. Freed blacks would now have to take care of themselves. Many former slave owners welcomed the chance to drive older blacks or trouble-makers from their plantations.

Planters, however, needed the labor of healthy men and women. Sooner or later, most freedmen returned to lands at or near their former homes. Once they arrived, planters wanted to ensure that they would not leave again.

Southern legislatures passed Black Codes. These racist laws were designed to restrict the activities of the former slaves. White Southerners were used to being able to keep their slaves in line with laws and threats. The Black Codes, set up in the years after the Civil War, would attempt to impose the same limits on the freedmen.

Black Codes denied African Americans the right to enter schools, theaters, hotels, and other public facilities. Black Codes all but forced freedmen back to plantations. A South Carolina law prohibited black people from taking any job other than agricultural or domestic work, unless they obtained a special license from the local judge. That license could cost from ten to one hundred dollars—a fortune for a postwar worker. A South Carolina code stated that, in contracts, "persons of color shall be known as servants and those with whom they contract shall be known as masters."[1]

In Opelousas, Louisiana, African Americans needed written permission from an employer to enter the city. No freedman could rent or keep a house there unless employed by a white person who would be responsible for his or her conduct. Each January, Mississippi required blacks to have written evidence of employment for the coming year. A laborer leaving his or her job before the end of the harvest season could forfeit any wages already earned for the year. He or she could also be arrested by any white person. Many Southern states had vagrancy laws; blacks who had no employer could be arrested. If they lacked money to pay a fine, they could be sent to work off the debt at a local farm. Apprenticeship laws produced a labor supply of young black workers for white planters. Laws allowed judges to bind black orphans or those with parents deemed unfit to white farmers.

In 1866, the United States government passed the Civil Rights Act. This law gave all citizens rights, regardless of race. Blacks could now make and enforce contracts, own and sell property, and file lawsuits in

BE IT ENACTED, THAT ALL PERSONS BORN IN THE UNITED STATES AND NOT SUBJECT TO ANY FOREIGN POWER, EXCLUDING INDIANS NOT TAXED, ARE HEREBY DECLARED TO BE CITIZENS OF THE UNITED STATES; AND SUCH CITIZENS, OF EVERY RACE AND COLOR, WITHOUT REGARD TO ANY PREVIOUS CONDITION OF SLAVERY OR INVOLUNTARY SERVITUDE, . . . SHALL HAVE THE SAME RIGHT, IN EVERY STATE AND TERRITORY IN THE UNITED STATES, TO MAKE AND ENFORCE CONTRACTS, TO SUE, BE PARTIES, AND GIVE EVIDENCE, TO INHERIT, PURCHASE, LEASE, SELL, HOLD, AND CONVEY REAL AND PERSONAL PROPERTY, AND TO FULL AND EQUAL BENEFIT OF ALL LAWS AND PROCEEDINGS FOR THE SECURITY OF PERSON AND PROPERTY, AS IS ENJOYED BY WHITE CITIZENS. . . .[2]

The Radical Republicans of Congress, who fought to support the rights of the former slaves, passed the Civil Rights Act in 1866.

court. President Johnson vetoed the bill, but both houses of Congress overrode his veto. It became law.

Congress extended the life of a major agency over another Johnson veto. The Bureau of Refugees, Freedmen, and Abandoned Lands, known as the Freedmen's Bureau, tried to ease the transition of former slaves to free life. It provided food, shelter, medical care, and education. The bureau set up more than four thousand schools throughout the South. It also sent hundreds of agents to help blacks find jobs. Despite its success in establishing schools, the under-manned Freedmen's Bureau was short-lived. Few agents had the ability or knowledge to deal with freed-men's problems. The bureau was disbanded in 1872.

Reconstruction

In 1867, Congress passed the Reconstruction Act, which divided the South into five military zones, each under a major general. President Johnson vetoed the bill, but Congress once again overrode his veto. The purpose of the Reconstruction Act was to supervise the return of Southern states to the Union. In theory, the act would allow for federal officers to help set up new governments for the South and to make sure that the civil rights of the former slaves were protected as they made the transition to freedom.

Under the Reconstruction Act, new elections would be held. Black men could vote in these elec-tions. After the elections, Southern states would draw up new constitutions that were acceptable to Congress.

The Freedmen's Bureau, depicted by an artist in this cartoon, tried to stand up for African Americans against Southern whites who wanted to prevent the former slaves from exercising their newly won civil rights.

The new state constitutions would have to allow blacks to vote. Only then could a former Confederate state reenter the Union. Interestingly, despite this requirement, a number of Northern states at the time also refused to allow blacks the right to vote.

Not all white men, most of whom had fought in the Confederate Army, reregistered to vote. Some, in fact, were not permitted to do so. As a result, 703,000 blacks registered in Southern states, compared with only 660,000 whites. Blacks formed the majority of voters in Alabama, Florida, Louisiana, South Carolina, and Mississippi.

Although whites tried to stop blacks from exercising this newly gained right, the large black registration to vote showed results. Men who had been slaves a few years earlier became legislators. In some states, they became lieutenant governors or secretaries of state. Sixteen African Americans were elected to Congress. In 1870, Mississippi's Hiram Revels became the first black United States senator. Four years later, fellow Mississippian Blanche K. Bruce joined him.

Revels, Bruce, and most other blacks joined the Republican party. This was the party of Abraham Lincoln, the president who had freed the slaves. Some whites in the South also joined the Republicans. They became known as scalawags. White Southerners who remained loyal to the Democratic party despised the Republicans.

The Reconstruction era provided for more than black votes. Congress, fearing that the Supreme Court might declare the Civil Rights Act unconstitutional, introduced the Fourteenth Amendment in 1868. This amendment granted full citizenship to all people born or naturalized in the United States, including blacks. Southern states would have objected to this amendment. However, they had not yet been readmitted into the Union. The Republican-controlled Congress would not allow states to reenter until they agreed to the Fourteenth Amendment.

Seven years later, the 1875 Civil Rights Act forbade discrimination in hotels, railways, theaters, and other private businesses providing public services. Those who did not comply faced serious fines and prison terms.

Ku Klux Klan

On Christmas Eve, 1865, six young men in Pulaski, Tennessee, formed a club called the Ku Klux Klan. Southern supporter Claude Bowers claimed, "the Klan was organized for the protection of women, property, civilization itself."[3] Because Southern whites could no longer legally dominate blacks, the Ku Klux Klan attempted to do so with fear.

Soon, the Tennessee club spread throughout the South. Hooded night riders dressed like ghosts spread *"a nameless terror* among negroes, poor whites," and Republicans.[4] By 1870, other similar organizations had formed. Raiders burned black schools and churches. They whipped or murdered African Americans and their white allies. They threatened blacks who tried to register to vote or demanded civil rights.

Klansmen attacked for a variety of reasons. In 1869, they lynched (killed) a freedman and his wife who were accused of "resenting a blow from his employer."[5] A black man named Andrew Flowers was whipped in 1870 after defeating a white candidate in an election. Flowers commented, "They said they had nothing particular against me, that they didn't dispute I was a very good fellow . . . but they did not intend any nigger to hold office in the United States."[6]

Opponents of the Klan fought back. Many of the men from Blount County in northern Alabama had fought for the Union in the Civil War. After the war, these veterans formed an anti-Klan organization. They threatened retaliation unless Klan members stopped whipping Union sympathizers and burning African-American properties.

In 1871, Congress passed the Ku Klux Klan act, or Force Bill. It gave the president the authority to use federal troops against the Klan. It made violent acts by the Klan and other terrorist groups punishable under federal law. This meant that juries composed of Unionists, not sympathetic white Southerners, would determine Klan members' innocence or guilt. Although the anti-Klan laws led to only a few hundred prosecutions, the Ku Klux Klan was stopped—at least temporarily.

This political cartoon by Thomas Nast shows how the many white supremacist groups that formed after the Civil War worked together to keep African Americans in a state of fear and poverty.

The End of Reconstruction

Most Southern whites resented Reconstruction. Some historians later referred to the period as "The Tragic Era."[7] By the mid-1870s, the North was growing tired of military rule over the former Confederacy. Besides, Northern industrialists wanted Southern markets and trade. They believed business could thrive better if the South were not under military rule.

In 1876, the presidential election led to changes in the South. Republican Rutherford B. Hayes, governor of Ohio, ran against Samuel Tilden, the Democratic governor of New York. At first, it appeared that the Democrat had won. Tilden had 4,287,670 popular votes, compared with 4,035,924 for Hayes. However, the winning candidate needed a majority of electoral votes. Tilden was one electoral vote short.

By this time, the former Confederate states had rejoined the Union. Federal troops remained only in Florida, Louisiana, and South Carolina. All three states at first gave majorities to Tilden. But Republican-dominated election boards canceled many Democratic votes in those states. The boards declared Hayes the winner in all three. Democrats protested this apparent fraud.

Congress created a special election panel to determine the winner. At first, the panel was made up of seven Democrats, seven Republicans, and one independent. Shortly before the panel was to meet, the independent resigned. A Republican replaced him.

The panel's vote followed party lines. Rutherford Hayes became the nineteenth president.

Southern Democrats reportedly made a deal. In exchange for not contesting the election further, Hayes would withdraw the remaining troops from the South. Whether or not there actually was a deal, Democrats kept silent and Hayes withdrew the troops.[8]

Without the federal troops, Southern blacks had little protection. Southern whites who called themselves Redeemers began to take over power. They hoped to restore the South to what it once was—a society divided by race in which the whites had all the power and blacks were forced to carry out the whites' will. After the end of Reconstruction, life in the South became a caste system. Birth determined destiny. The most educated and accomplished black person would rank lower than the poorest white.

In 1883, the United States Supreme Court ruled the 1875 Civil Rights Act unconstitutional. It declared that the Fourteenth Amendment did not allow Congress to pass laws prohibiting discrimination in privately owned businesses. John Harlan, a former slave owner, cast the only dissenting vote. Harlan wrote that the decision of his eight colleagues reduced the Fourteenth Amendment to "splendid baubles, thrown out to delude those who deserved fair and generous treatment at the hands of the nation."[9]

African-American writer and activist Frederick Douglass declared the ruling a disaster. He feared it would leave blacks with no legal defense: "They can put [an African American] in a smoking car or baggage car . . . take him or leave him from all places of amusement or instruction, without the least fear that the National Government will interfere for the protection of his liberty."[10]

For the most part, the governments of Southern states lived up to Douglass's fears. The age of Jim Crow would soon be under way.

Traveling performer Thomas "Daddy" Rice needed a new act for his 1820s show. One day, he saw a raggedly dressed elderly black man dancing. Rice borrowed the man's clothes, blackened his own face, and then performed a ridiculous shuffling dance. Rice sang, "Wheelabout and turn about and jump just so, every time I wheel about I jump Jim Crow."[1] Rice's act was a crude mockery of blacks. But white audiences in both the South and the North made the act a huge success. Soon the term *Jim Crow*, referring to African Americans, became part of America's vocabulary.

LIFE UNDER JIM CROW

"Jim Crow" laws passed in the late 1800s greatly limited blacks' freedom. After a while, the term *Jim Crow* became more than a set of laws. It referred to a way of life that was full of limitations for African Americans. In some ways, these humiliations were as bad as slavery.

"Colored Water and White Water"

In 1900, 10 million whites and 6 million blacks shared the eleven states that made up the former Confederate

South. They saw and worked with each other every day. But in some respects, they might as well have lived on different planets.

Jim Crow laws separated blacks from whites in schools, public transportation, hospitals, and orphanages. Even death did not end this segregation. Blacks had separate funeral homes and separate cemeteries.

Signs reading "white only" or "colored only" proclaimed Jim Crow facilities everywhere. They showed up in washrooms, parks, hotels, and restaurants. In some places, such as post offices or banks, whites and blacks shared facilities. However, blacks had to wait until whites were finished before they could be served. The Reverend Ernest Whitehead commented, "We had colored fountains to drink out of, and white fountains. We had colored water and white water."[2]

Houses of worship, which had often been segregated in both the North and the South in the years before the Civil War, especially reflected the racial divisions of the Jim Crow era. A white deacon in a Mississippi church saw an unknown black man in the church building. "Boy, what you doin' in there?" he asked. "Don't you know this is a white church?"

"Boss, I only just got here to mop up the floor," the black man answered.

The white man thought a minute. "Well, that's all right then," he answered. "But don't let me catch you prayin'."[3]

"There Were to Be *No* Victories"

Life in the South had become a caste system. Anyone who was born black, no matter how high the person's education or abilities, had fewer rights than the poorest white. "We came to know that whatever we had was always inferior," noted author Pauli Murray. "We came to understand that no matter how neat and clean, how law abiding churchgoing and moral . . . it made no essential difference in our own place."[4]

Whites kept blacks from voting, oppressed them through the legal system, and abused them in many different ways. They cheated blacks out of their earnings. This was easy to do, considering that poorly educated blacks had little ability to read or negotiate fair contracts. Whites also assured that they would have a labor supply by passing vagrancy laws that could imprison blacks on trivial charges. Whites tried to justify this treatment by claiming that they knew what was best for blacks.

Those who defied white oppression faced blacklists, court charges, or vigilante "justice." "The laws were so rigid no one could ever think you could break them," recalled black journalist Vernon Jarrett.[5] "There were to be *no* [black] victories."[6]

Knowing One's Place

A set of written and unwritten rules governed relations between whites and blacks in the South. These were intended to keep a black person in his or her place—in a social position below that of a white person.

SEC. 2.... ALL FREEDMEN, FREE NEGROES AND MULATTOES IN THIS STATE, OVER THE AGE OF EIGHTEEN YEARS, FOUND ON THE SECOND MONDAY IN JANUARY, 1866, OR THEREAFTER, WITH NO LAWFUL EMPLOYMENT OR BUSINESS, OR FOUND UNLAWFULLY ASSEMBLING THEMSELVES TOGETHER, EITHER IN THE DAY OR NIGHT TIME, AND ALL WHITE PERSONS SO ASSEMBLING THEMSELVES WITH FREEDMEN, FREE NEGROES OR MULATTOES, ON TERMS OF EQUALITY, OR LIVING IN ADULTERY OR FORNICATION WITH A FREED WOMAN, FREE NEGRO OR MULATTO, SHALL BE DEEMED VAGRANTS, AND ON CONVICTION THEREOF SHALL BE FINED . . . AND IMPRISONED. . . .[7]

Black Codes restricted the freedom of African Americans, essentially keeping them in a state of slavery. This is a vagrancy law passed by the state of Mississippi after the Civil War.

Black and white children often played together in the South. But by the teenage years, their carefree friendships ended. From then on, the white person would be dominant, the black submissive. Blacks were expected to address whites as "mister," "missus," or "miss." Whites addressed blacks as "boy" or "girl." Older blacks were called "uncle" or "auntie."

If white people walked along a sidewalk, blacks had to step aside and let them pass. Black drivers could not pass whites who were driving a buggy. A black man was expected to take off his hat when a white person came near. He did not start a conversation with a white person.

Southern blacks learned early in life to curb their ambitions. "I could never aspire to be President of the United States or governor of my state," wrote author Alben Hosley. "I knew that front doors of white homes in my town were not for me to enter, except as a servant."[8]

Many Southern whites resented any kind of black success. They accused blacks who appeared well-to-do of being "uppity." Civil rights leader Benjamin Mays recalled that a white man struck him when he was young for "trying to look too good."[9]

Many blacks hid their prosperity. Some did not paint their houses even though they could afford to do so. They bought items from mail order catalogs, so local white merchants would not discover their prosperity. Industrious black Southerners who bought cars risked having them destroyed by jealous whites.

Any black man caught, or suspected of, having sexual relations with a white woman would almost certainly die. Death might be the sentence of a court as a result of rape charges, or it might come at the hands of a lynch mob. White men, on the other hand, had little fear of the law after attacking a black woman.

One man who posed a huge threat to whites was Jack Johnson. The African-American boxer defeated a white Australian to win the heavyweight championship in 1908. Two years later, white promoters found a "great white hope" to challenge Johnson.[10] They lured former boxing champion James J. Jeffries out of retirement. Johnson pummeled the out-of-shape Jeffries to retain the title. The fight created such racial tension that there were race riots in some cities.

Johnson's victories were a blow to whites' pride. But the black fighter added insult to injury. He was cocky, arrogant, and disrespectful of his white opponents. Worst of all, in the eyes of Southern whites, he openly traveled with a white woman.

To black America, Jack Johnson was a hero. Many whites detested him. Although Southern blacks rejoiced among themselves at Johnson's success, they knew better than to mention the fighter's name near a white man. White disgust with Johnson became so great that Congress outlawed transporting boxing films between states in the hopes of preventing black Southerners from viewing their hero in action.

"This Plantation Is a Place for Me to Make a Profit"

After the Civil War, newly freed blacks often dreamed of "forty acres and a mule."[11] During Reconstruction, Republican government officials had briefly offered former slaves parcels of land to help them become free workers. The reality was far different—and far harsher. For most blacks, the independence and land ownership they craved turned out to be an illusion.

Blacks had few options other than farm work. Industries such as textiles, furniture, and paper were growing in the South. But whites kept blacks from those industries. Many slaves had learned the skills to become successful artisans. White craftsmen, however, openly discouraged black competition for what they considered "White men's work."[12]

African Americans did not have the choice of not working. Every Southern state passed vagrancy laws, which punished those who had no job. Although the laws themselves were color-blind, enforcement was not. An unemployed white man might be the lovable town loafer. An unemployed black might find himself in jail.

For black farm workers, life was a series of crises. Thunderstorms, tornadoes, or floods could ravage the land. In the early 1910s, an insect called the boll weevil entered the South from Mexico. The weevil devoured crops and did millions of dollars' worth of damage. But the greatest problems blacks faced were human-made, not natural ones.

African Americans did not have much choice about their jobs during the Jim Crow era. By law, they had to work, and many ended up doing farm work, often on the same plantations some had worked as slaves.

Black workers after the Civil War were not slaves. But in many ways, their conditions differed little from those of slavery. Whites forced blacks to sign labor contracts every year. The contracts usually forced blacks to work from sunrise to sunset six days a week. Workers could not leave the plantation for any reason without the planter's permission. Employers could enter a worker's home at any time. Workers could be fined for being absent or for anything the employer considered misbehavior.

White planters and businessmen were the ones who totaled the money. More often than not, they cheated the blacks. If a black person earned a substantial sum for his or her labor, whites would claim that the black owed additional expenses. These costs would take away the rest of the black person's money. Black workers took their lives in their hands if they protested unfair white accounting.

African-American women in the Southern states worked at least as hard as men did. Many toiled alongside their husbands or fathers in the cotton fields, in addition to doing household chores. Other women worked as domestic servants in white people's homes, where they prepared meals, cleaned house, and washed clothes and dishes. If they were lucky, they could return home before dark and do their own chores there. In most cases, the black workers also had families of their own to care for.

"Three Days for Stealing, Eighty-seven Days for Being Colored"

Farm life was hard, but the usual alternative was much worse. Every year, thousands of African Americans were arrested, convicted, and imprisoned.

"Equal justice under the law" was a joke in Southern courts. It was said that more blacks went to jail for stealing a farm animal than whites did for killing a black man. Blacks, particularly young men, often found themselves arrested for gambling, vagrancy, or other minor charges. A New Orleans newspaper claimed that a black defendant received ninety days in jail: "three days for stealing, eighty-seven days for being colored."[13]

The sentence might depend less on what the accused did than on whom he or she knew. If the black defendant had a white sponsor who would speak for him or her, the defendant might escape with little or no punishment. If there were no such sponsor, the convicted person might end up on a prison farm.

Convict labor was more than a means of punishment for black (and some poor white) prisoners. It became a profitable business for the Southern states. They leased prisoners to white employers for use as plantation and factory workers. In the 1880s, Tennessee and Alabama each received about $100,000 for their inmates' services, a huge sum at the time. States made money from these prisoners in many ways. In Tennessee, state officials sold the urine of inmates to tanneries. Unclaimed bodies of deceased black prisoners often went to universities for research by medical students.

Few convicts who were sentenced to ten or more years survived their terms. Planters and business owners had no reason to treat the prisoners well. A dead prisoner could easily be replaced. If there were a shortage of convict workers, local police would round up young, powerless blacks on petty charges. They became the new convict labor force.

Lynching

Those who were merely jailed were sometimes the lucky ones. In the late nineteenth and early twentieth centuries, thousands of innocent blacks paid for white racism with their lives.

Whites lynched hundreds of African Americans every year. Lynching means killing without first holding a trial, as punishment for an alleged offense. In 1910, 846 lynchings were recorded. From 1890 until 1917, on average, two to three blacks in the South were illegally hanged, burned, or otherwise murdered every week.[14]

Often, these killings took place off quiet roads in the country. At times, however, the executions became public events. Trains brought spectators to an execution. Vendors sold ice cream and lemonade at hangings.

Lynchings took place with little or no objection from white authorities. Any sheriff who tried to arrest a lyncher knew he would face strong opposition at

The lynching of an African American was considered entertainment to many Southern whites. Often, huge crowds would gather to watch the violent spectacle.

election time. Besides, even if a lyncher were arrested, there would likely be no witnesses willing to come forward. Blacks, fearing a similar fate, were afraid to testify against someone charged with lynching. Those whites who opposed lynching feared the wrath of their neighbors. Even white ministers hesitated to speak out against lynching.

Sometimes a minor crime would lead to a lynching. More often, though, the victims had somehow violated an unwritten racial code. Owning too much property, trying to register to vote, demanding full value for one's labor—any of these "offenses" could lead to the wrong end of a noose.

Lynch mobs sometimes executed people other than those they were seeking. To many, the victim's identity was of little importance. A black person was executed as a warning to others, not as a means of justice.

Birth of a Nation

Negative feelings about blacks were not confined to the South. A 1915 film brought racial issues before the entire nation. Southerner D. W. Griffith produced *Birth of a Nation* in 1915. Film historian Donald Bogle described it as "a legendary classic. . . . Technically innovative and sweeping." Bogle also called it "a racist masterpiece." He claimed "the treatment of its black characters has also made this the most controversial American film ever released."[15] Set during Reconstruction, *Birth of a Nation* glorified Southern whites and demeaned blacks. The black characters were scheming politicians or physical brutes. They drank whiskey, made foolish laws, and threatened white women. Finally, when all appeared lost for the whites, hope appeared. The Ku Klux Klan came to the rescue.

Birth of a Nation was a huge success. White audiences, in the North as well as the South, cheered the hooded raiders. Thanks largely to the movie, the Klan saw a revival in the 1920s. It gained substantial membership in states as far north as Indiana. The revived Klan was no less ruthless than the orginal.

"A Private Inner Dignity"

How did blacks survive day after day, year after year, despite continual physical, mental, and spiritual abuse? They endured thanks to resources in their own community. First and foremost were their families and the black churches. Pastors in these churches did more than preach. A minister might be a teacher, job counselor, recreational director, babysitter, and informal legal advisor.

Whites seldom let blacks into their clubs, so blacks formed their own. Religious, social, and fraternal societies sprung up in the South. These groups performed services for the black community and served as a source of community pride.

A rich tradition of oral communication preserved a unique African-American culture. Blacks expressed thoughts, hopes, and opinions in many different ways. They relayed the horrors of slavery and the humor of life in folk tales. They made labor more bearable with work songs. Religious feelings flowed through gospel songs and sermons.

Black creativity surfaced in many forms of music. But perhaps no form was more expressive than the blues. A blues song could be sad, joyful, or thoughtful. Blues could deal with any subject—work, lost loves, gambling, religion, liquor, politics, boll weevils, racism, floods, and music itself. Blues music survives today. Its influence can be seen in such musical forms as country and rock and roll.

Most of all, blacks survived with inner powers that defied explanation. "Servants maintained a private inner dignity despite a life that was saturated with indignity," claimed Vernon Jarrett. "My father spent his whole life being considered a second-class citizen. Yet he and my mother taught for a combined one hundred years. People like them radiated pride. I've never had so much admiration for spiritual strength."[16]

"SEPARATE BUT EQUAL"

An 1890 Louisiana statute segregated races on trains. Passengers could enter only those cars assigned to their own race. The Louisiana train law was not unusual in the South, but it was particularly notable. Blacks and whites had lived in relative harmony in New Orleans. The city had many residents of mixed blood. These creoles were often quite wealthy. Before the Civil War, some had owned slaves.

Louisiana's 1890 law posed a threat to the security of these relatively well-off citizens. They decided to fight the act. Louis Martinet, a black lawyer and newspaper man, took action. He gathered sixteen other black Louisianans and formed the Citizens Committee to Test the Constitutionality of the Separate Car Law. On October 10, 1891, the committee hired lawyer James A. Walker to handle the case in Louisiana courts. Albion Tourgee, a white attorney from Ohio, would argue the case if it went to the United States Supreme Court.

Daniel F. Desdunes, the son of a committee member, volunteered to be arrested and brought to court.

Separate facilities for whites and blacks were the rule in many places throughout the Jim Crow era. This photograph, taken during the Great Depression in the 1930s, shows that segregated theaters were still common even after the turn of the twentieth century.

The court, however, dismissed his case. Desdunes had bought a ticket for a destination outside of Louisiana. The Louisiana Supreme Court ruled that the law did not apply to interstate travel.

The committee then selected Homer Plessy. This time, it made sure the rider had a destination in Louisiana. It is possible that the train company knew about and approved of this action. After all, the law was costing train companies money. Extra cars placed on a train to preserve segregation cost money, even if those cars were not first-class accommodations.

Martinet expressed confidence that a court would strike down the discriminatory law. "Jim Crow is dead as a door nail," he predicted.[1]

On June 7, 1892, Homer Plessy boarded a car reserved for whites on the East Louisiana Railway. When he refused to leave, Plessy was arrested and taken to the local jail. The case went before Judge John H. Ferguson of the criminal court of the Parish of New Orleans. Walker claimed the decisions against Plessy were unfair on several grounds. First, the law itself was unclear. It was unclear where light-skinned blacks belonged. Second, the lawyer said the law gave unwarranted powers to train conductors, who had to determine the race of passengers. Finally, Plessy's lawyers claimed that the law violated the Fourteenth Amendment, because it put blacks in a lesser position in society. Plessy's lawyer charged that the segregation law was passed in order to promote the comfort of whites only, not the "general comfort" specified in the law. After all, black nurses were allowed on "whites only" cars—if they were taking care of white passengers. The state's attorneys argued that the law was created to avoid fights between blacks and whites in railroad cars.

That November, Judge Ferguson ruled against Plessy. The *New Orleans Times-Picayune* commented, "It is hoped that what [Judge Ferguson] says will have some effect on the silly negroes who are trying to fight this law. The sooner they drop their so-called crusade against 'the Jim Crow car' . . . the better for them."[2]

Plessy's attorneys expected this loss. They likewise were expecting defeat in the Louisiana Supreme Court. After all, Chief Justice Francis Nicholls was the former governor who had signed the segregation bill into law. He and the other justices upheld the Louisiana law in December 1892. Justice Charles Fenner said it was not discriminatory because whites, as well as blacks, could not enter the other race's car. He did not mention that few, if any, whites would want to go to an inferior facility.

Tourgee planned to appeal the case to the United States Supreme Court. But he was in no hurry to do so. Tourgee commented to Martinet in 1893 that at least five justices were opposed to their cause. Only Justice John Harlan appeared to favor blacks' rights. Besides, appeals cost money. Tourgee and his allies had to continue fund-raising efforts.

Tourgee submitted the case to the United States Supreme Court in 1895. It was argued on April 13,

IF THE TWO RACES ARE TO MEET UPON TERMS OF SOCIAL EQUALITY, IT MUST BE THE RESULT OF NATURAL AFFINITIES, A MUTUAL APPRECIATION OF EACH OTHER'S MERITS, AND A VOLUNTARY CONSENT OF INDIVIDUALS. [LEGISLATION] IS POWERLESS TO ERADICATE RACIAL INSTINCTS, OR TO ABOLISH DISTINCTIONS BASED UPON PHYSICAL DIFFER-ENCES, AND THE ATTEMPT TO DO SO CAN ONLY RESULT IN ACCENTUATING THE DIFFICULTIES OF THE PRESENT SITUATION. IF THE CIVIL AND POLITICAL RIGHTS OF BOTH RACES BE EQUAL, ONE CANNOT BE INFERIOR TO THE OTHER CIVILLY OR POLITICALLY. IF ONE RACE BE INFERIOR TO THE OTHER SOCIALLY, THE CONSTITUTION OF THE UNITED STATES CANNOT PUT THEM UPON THE SAME PLANE. . . .[3]

In the 1896 case Plessy v. Ferguson, *the United States Supreme Court accepted the idea of "separate but equal" facilities for whites and blacks.*

1896. A month later, the Court announced its decision. By a 7–1 vote, it upheld the Louisiana law.

Judge Henry Billings Brown wrote the majority opinion. Biographer Francis A. Helminski claimed that Brown held a low opinion of blacks, women, Jews, and immigrants. Brown said that blacks and whites should have equal facilities, but "If one race be inferior to the other socially, the Constitution of the United States cannot put them upon the same plane."[4]

Harlan, the Kentucky-born former slave owner, cast the dissenting vote. "There is no caste system here," he wrote. "Our Constitution is color blind and neither knows nor tolerates classes among citizens. In respect to civil rights, all citizens are equal before the law."[5] He added, "The thin disguise of 'equal' accommodations for passengers in railroad coaches will not mislead anyone, nor atone for the wrong this day done."[6]

Despite his upbringing in the South, Justice John Harlan wrote a bitter dissenting opinion to the Plessy *case in which he spoke up for equal rights for African Americans.*

Homer Plessy paid the twenty-five-dollar fine, then disappeared into history. His name lives on in a decision that influenced the nation for half a century. The doctrine that emerged from *Plessy* v. *Ferguson* became known as separate but equal. Blacks could be kept apart from whites, as long as both races had comparable facilities. Southern governments strictly enforced the "separate." They all but ignored the "equal."

Booker T. Washington had reason to be nervous on September 18, 1895. The young college president was about to give a major speech. He would address the Cotton States and International Exposition in Atlanta. He gave the speech as though he were speaking

5

ACTION OR ACCOMMODATION

to other blacks. However, the speech was really directed to whites. "Cast down your bucket where you are," he said, advising blacks not to leave the farms where they worked.[1] He also advised blacks not to worry about segregation: "In all things that are purely social we can be as separate as the five fingers, yet one as the hand in all things essential to mutual progress."[2] This speech was widely quoted. It helped make Washington a national figure and black spokesman.

Washington believed that, through hard work and economic achievement, blacks could achieve equal status with whites. The formula had worked for him. Born to a slave woman and an unknown white man, he took the surname Washington after George Washington. When his mother told him that whites discouraged blacks from reading, he became determined to learn how to read and write. At age sixteen, after working

Booker T. Washington was one of the most influential African-American leaders during the Jim Crow era.

several jobs, he walked five hundred miles to attend Hampton Institute in Virginia.

Hampton was the nation's leading industrial (vocational) school for blacks. Washington appreciated his time there. In 1881, he became president of a small industrial school in Tuskegee, Alabama. Washington worked to make the Tuskegee Institute follow the Hampton model. Tuskegee had only two small buildings and a few teachers when Washington took over. His work turned it into the largest black institution in the country. By 1906, it would have fifteen hundred students and a staff of five hundred.

The institute did not teach fine arts, philosophy, or languages. Instead, Tuskegee taught male students to become blacksmiths, bricklayers, or carpenters. The school improved farming skills. George Washington Carver, the nation's leading agricultural scientist, taught there. Women took classes in cooking and sewing.

Washington's school taught social skills such as cleanliness, promptness, good manners, and character building. It also taught blacks to show proper respect to whites, obey contracts, and respect private property. These were the lessons Washington considered necessary to get along in a white-dominated world.

Booker T. Washington's influence showed in more than Tuskegee. In 1900, he founded the National Negro Business League. This group offered funds and advice to help black businesses prosper, In many cases, the league was very helpful. In 1900, there were only

ONE-THIRD OF THE POPULATION OF THE SOUTH IS OF THE NEGRO RACE. NO ENTERPRISE SEEKING THE MATERIAL, CIVIL, OR MORAL WELFARE OF THIS SECTION CAN DISREGARD THIS ELEMENT OF OUR POPULATION AND REACH THE HIGHEST SUCCESS. . . .

TO THOSE OF MY RACE WHO DEPEND ON BETTERING THEIR CONDITION IN A FOREIGN LAND OR WHO UNDERESTIMATE THE IMPORTANCE OF CULTIVATING FRIENDLY RELATIONS WITH THE SOUTHERN WHITE MAN, WHO IS THEIR NEXT-DOOR NEIGHBOUR, I WOULD SAY: "CAST DOWN YOUR BUCKET WHERE YOU ARE"—CAST IT DOWN IN MAKING FRIENDS IN EVERY MANLY WAY OF THE PEOPLE OF ALL RACES BY WHOM WE ARE SURROUNDED.[3]

Booker T. Washington's "Cast Down Your Bucket" speech helped make him a national figure in the struggle to uplift African Americans.

four black-owned banks. That number grew to fifty-six in 1911.

"One of the Most Wonderful Men"

The lessons and philosophy of Tuskegee were what Booker T. Washington explained in his Atlanta speech. For the next twenty years, he would repeat the same themes thousands of times in articles and speeches. He stressed industrial education, self-help, and good character. Only with economic strength, Washington claimed, would blacks gain respect and power from whites.

Washington practiced what became known as accommodation. He did whatever had to be done to get along with whites. He seldom wasted an opportunity to praise anything whites did to help African Americans. He largely kept publicly silent about injustices. He told blacks that their best friends were the "better class" of whites.[4] However, he often criticized other blacks. His speeches mentioned black responsibilities but seldom black rights. He occasionally told "darkie" stories, using negative racial stereotypes. He once wrote, "There was much in slavery besides its hardships and cruelties, much that was tender, human, and beautiful."[5]

Some leading African Americans in the early 1900s called for voting rights and an end to segregation. Booker T. Washington was not one of them. He did not oppose literacy tests for would-be black voters, as long as those standards also applied to whites. Nor did he speak out against laws that kept blacks out of restaurants or first-class train cars. Washington himself was not a victim of these injustices. He traveled in first-class train cars with white passengers. While Alabama kept almost all blacks from the ballot box, Washington and other Tuskegee leaders were allowed to register and vote. This new breed of blacks seemed nonthreatening to Southern whites.

Washington was honored after the 1895 speech. Harvard University gave him an honorary doctorate in 1896. He became the first African American to be so awarded. President Theodore Roosevelt invited him to dine at the White House in 1901. Roosevelt made Washington his unofficial advisor on black affairs. Roosevelt and successor William Howard Taft followed Washington's recommendations on black political appointments. Washington's autobiography, *Up from Slavery*, became a best-seller.

Northern donors turned to the Tuskegee president. Oil tycoon John D. Rockefeller donated to the university. Steel magnate Andrew Carnegie gave $600,000 in bonds. Carnegie described Washington as "certainly one of the most wonderful men living or who has ever lived."[6]

Washington shared the philanthropic spoils. He recommended white donations to other schools, but only those that shared his philosophies.

Washington also had great power in the black press. He often claimed it would be improper for him to run a newspaper (even though he was part owner of the influential *New York Age*). However, he was known to make generous "donations" (critics would call them bribes) to papers that supported his views.

There was another side to Washington that the public did not see. He secretly funneled thousands of dollars to help court cases on issues such as black voting rights and the right of blacks to serve on juries. He quietly helped a lobbyist block a bill that would have allowed railroad segregation in the North.

When Booker T. Washington died in 1915, he received a great deal of praise. But his philosophy of accommodation to whites largely died with him. Although some might have regretted the passing of the man, few mourned his philosophy. If he expected white approval of black economic advancement, he was mistaken. Jim Crow was just as alive in 1915 as it had been in 1895.

Fighting "the Rope and the Torch"

Thomas Moss, Calvin McDowell, and Henry Stewart typified Booker T. Washington's philosophy. They worked hard and led clean lives. The three owned the People's Grocery in a Memphis, Tennessee, suburb. This new grocery cut into the business of a white-owned store.

In 1893, a group of boys was playing marbles in front of a store. A squabble among the boys grew into a fight involving black and white adults. Police arrested the three grocers. A mob seized them in jail, then murdered the three outside of town.

The killings appalled a young African-American newspaper editor. Ida B. Wells of the Memphis *Free Speech* had been a friend of Moss's. She proclaimed, "He was murdered, with no more consideration than if he had been a dog, because he as a man defended his property from attack."[7]

Wells spoke out against the grocers' deaths and other lynchings in her paper. She became the most vocal critic of segregation in the 1890s. She wrote, "Nowhere in the civilized world save the United States of America do men, possessing all civil and political power, go out in bands of 50 to 5,000 to hunt down, hang, or burn to death a single individual, unarmed and absolutely powerless."[8] When Wells refused to retract her statements, white supremacists destroyed her newspaper office.

Wells formed the African-American Council in 1899. This group stressed action rather than accommodation. The organization criticized Booker T. Washington for statements it claimed seemed to excuse lynchings. Washington's tactics alienated many black leaders, including his most influential rival.

In 1895, William Edward Burghardt (W.E.B.) Du Bois became the first African American to earn a doctorate from Harvard. The following year, he published *The Suppression of the African Slave Trade to the United States of America, 1638–1870*, a study of efforts to stop the slave trade. In 1898, Du Bois became a professor of history and economics at Atlanta University. There, he organized an annual conference to discuss black

Ida B. Wells was the most outspoken opponent of lynching through the years of Jim Crow segregation.

problems. Unlike Washington, Du Bois stressed liberal arts at his university. He sought training for the "talented tenth," the most promising black students.[9]

Du Bois emerged as a leading Washington critic. He agreed with the idea of black self-help. But he believed that Washington's policies "practically accepted the alleged inferiority of the Negro."[10] Du Bois felt that blacks needed political rights in order to assure economic security.

In 1904, Washington, Du Bois, and other black leaders met in New York City's Carnegie Hall. Du Bois presented a list of demands: full political rights for blacks, higher education for selected black youth, a national black periodical, establishment of a defense fund, and a strong fight in the courts for civil rights. The convention, largely attended by Washington followers, rejected the platform. Du Bois left the conference, determined to form his own civil rights group.

The Niagara Movement

In 1905, Du Bois sent a letter to sixty black professionals, inviting them to a meeting at Niagara Falls. About thirty showed up.

The meeting led to the formation of the Niagara Movement. It called for an end to segregation, disfranchisement (lack of voting rights), and violence against blacks. The movement blamed white supremacists for black failures. Booker T. Washington's nonconfrontational philosophy was another target.

Washington did not take kindly to the criticism directed at him. He hired the Pinkerton detective agency to find information he could use to discredit Niagara members. He also bribed newspapers to ignore the meeting.

Unfortunately, the poorly financed Niagara Movement failed to attract working-class blacks or sympathetic whites. Within five years, the Niagara Movement disbanded. However, the effort was not entirely wasted. Black leaders made connections that would serve them in later struggles.

NAACP

In 1908, a race riot broke out in Springfield, Illinois. Race-based outbreaks were not unknown in Southern cities, but a riot in the Illinois capital made it very clear that racism had always existed in the North as well as in the South.

Among the shocked Northerners was white journalist Mary White Ovington. She organized a conference to deal with discrimination. In 1909, the National Negro Conference met in New York City. It led to the formation of the National Association for the Advancement of Colored People (NAACP). The NAACP set up headquarters in New York in 1910. W.E.B. Du Bois was named editor of the *Crisis*, the organization's newspaper. He was the only black leader active in the white-dominated organization.

The NAACP stressed legal action to correct existing evils. It sent investigators to record Southern atrocities

W.E.B. Du Bois became a powerful African-American leader, as well as a founding member of the NAACP.

in rural communities. One successful investigator was light-skinned, blue-eyed Walter White. A Georgia storekeeper told White, "Sheriffs and police and governors and prosecuting attorneys have got too much sense to mix in lynching-bees. If they do they know they might as well give up all idea of running for office any more—if something worse don't happen to them."[11]

Washington saw this new group as a threat to his power. As with the Niagara Movement, he sought to discredit the NAACP and its leaders. The NAACP, however, survived the attacks. After Washington's death, it attracted many of his former supporters.

By the time of Washington's death, African Americans had several ways of coping with white racism. Some followed Washington's accommodationist stance. Others supported the more activist NAACP. For thousands of blacks, there was a third solution. They left the South.

6

"COME NORTH"

Thousands of black Southerners stood at crowded railroad stations waiting for the Illinois Central and other northbound trains. Others waited miles away from the depot, at unmarked stops in the countryside. They knew it was dangerous to be seen leaving town.

They went for jobs that paid far more than those in the South. Some sought the bright lights and excitement of Chicago or New York. All went looking for freedom that was undreamed of in the land they were leaving behind.

"Not as Good as a White Man's Dog"

Between 1865 and 1890, about forty thousand blacks moved west to Kansas. About one hundred eighty-five thousand black migrants went north in the 1890s. Many of these were affluent and educated residents of border states like Tennessee and Virginia. People such as former Congressman George White and journalist Ida B. Wells went north. These were among the "talented tenth" that W.E.B. Du Bois had hoped would lead the black population in the South.

They often moved to cities. By 1900, six cities—New York, Philadelphia, Baltimore, Washington, Memphis, and New Orleans—had at least fifty thousand black inhabitants. More than one quarter of African Americans were living in urban areas.

Those who left the farms could give many reasons for doing so. "There were no jobs, no education there," claimed Margaret Burroughs, founder of Chicago's Du Sable Museum of African American History.[1] *The Houston Observer* claimed that the black Southerner "is kicked around, cuffed, lynched, burned, homes destroyed, daughters insulted and sometimes raped, has no vote or voice, and in some instances when he asks for pay receives a 2 x 4 over the head."[2] One Mississippi man said simply, "Down here a negro man is not as good as a white man's dog."[3]

Efforts to Keep Blacks in the South

Southern whites might have abused and mistreated their black neighbors. But they did not want them to leave the South. If they left, who would do the back-breaking, low-paying work? Poor whites would not stand jobs under slavelike conditions. Likewise, European immigrants to the United States refused to accept working conditions that were worse than those they left back home. Plantation owners maintained, "Negroes are a necessity to the South, and it is desirable that they should stay there and not migrate to the North."[4]

Whites tried different tactics to keep blacks from leaving the South. Some raised workers' pay. Others suggested reforms, such as an end to lynchings. Some pointed out bad weather, high rents, or low-quality food in the North. If an unhappy migrant returned from the North, Southern newspapers headlined his or her story.

Leading Southern blacks also cautioned blacks to stay at home. Booker T. Washington, fearing a loss of funds from his white supporters, urged blacks to stay on the farm. Many black doctors, lawyers, and ministers faced a loss of income if their most prosperous clients fled. They, too, spoke out against migration.

If rewards or bribery did not work, whites resorted to force. In Macon, Georgia, police ousted several hundred northbound blacks from the city's railroad station. In Americus, Georgia, local authorities boarded a train and arrested fifty blacks who were trying to leave. Stories like these alerted and frightened many black migrants. Often they left in the middle of the night, without notifying friends or neighbors. They caught the train miles from town to avoid detection by the local police or sheriff.

Many Northern companies sent labor agents to the South. These whites passed on information about jobs in Detroit, Chicago, and Cleveland. Southern whites often refused to believe that their own racism led to black flight. They blamed the labor agents as outside troublemakers who were spoiling blacks' happy lives in the South. By about 1917, labor agents were no longer needed. Letters from family and friends in the North provided better advertising than any stranger could give.

The *Defender*

Chicagoan Robert S. Abbott started his newspaper in 1905, with an investment of twenty-five cents. By 1915, his *Chicago Defender* had become the largest and most influential black-owned paper in the nation.

The *Defender* was published in Chicago, but two thirds of its circulation was outside of the city. African Americans throughout the South read news that white Southern papers refused, and that black papers were afraid, to print.

Abbott refused to use the term *Negroes*. His *Defender* was by and for "the race." Abbott's editorial rule was simple: If it could benefit the race, he printed it. He used every opportunity to attack Southern abuses. For a popular series, *Below the Mason Dixon Line*, he sent reporters into small Southern towns. Local people told racial horror stories, which the reporters relayed to the Chicago-based newspaper.

Not surprisingly, Southern white authorities hated and feared the *Defender*. They went to any lengths possible to stop its circulation. In some towns, a person could be arrested for distributing the *Defender*. But Abbott befriended railroad workers, who helped sneak the paper to willing readers. These copies would be passed around to friends and neighbors, sometimes until the ink smudged off the pages.

At first, Abbott advised blacks against moving. "The only thing to do is stick to the farm," he wrote.[5] But by 1916, the *Defender* had a new message: "Come North."[6]

The Great Migration

Events came together, in America and abroad, in 1915 and 1916. These events altered the United States' racial landscape.

The Southern agricultural economy depended on cotton, often the only profitable crop. Any misfortune to the cotton crop could mean disaster. When the boll weevil ruined much of the South's cotton crop in 1915, blacks and whites alike suffered. When new machines made work for owners easier—at the expense of black workers—longtime farm hands became unemployed. Where could they go?

They went to cities in the North. Around the turn of the twentieth century, millions of European immigrants were arriving in the United States. They took jobs in a rapidly expanding factory-based economy. But World War I, which began in 1914, was ravaging Europe. The war, which the United States entered in 1917, cut off a much-needed labor supply. Immigration had to stop, and eventually, most able-bodied white men were called to fight in the military. Employers looked elsewhere for a workforce. In the Southern black population, they found willing and able employees.

More than half a million Southern blacks made their way north between 1916 and 1919. Most headed

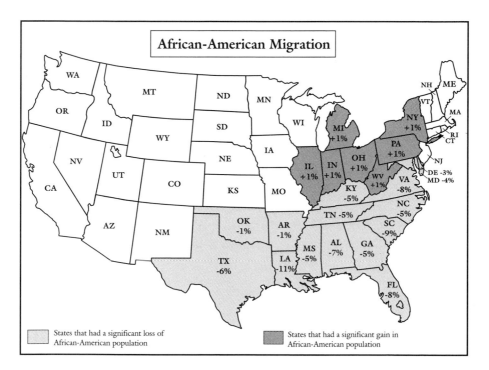

African-American Migration

WA

MT

OR

ID

WY

NV

UT

CA

AZ

NM

ND

SD

NE

CO

KS

MN

WI

IA

MO

OK
-1%

TX
-6%

AR
-1%

LA
-11%

MS
-5%

AL
-7%

GA
-5%

MI
+1%

IL
+1%

IN
+1%

OH
+1%

KY
-5%

TN -5%

WV
+1%

VA
-8%

NC
-5%

SC
-9%

FL
-8%

NH

ME

VT

NY
+1%

MA

RI

CT

PA
+1%

NJ

DE -3%

MD -4%

States that had a significant loss of
African-American population

States that had a significant gain in
African-American population

*The migration of massive numbers of African Americans
from the South to Northern cities dramatically changed the
populations of many areas of the country.*

for cities such as Chicago, Detroit, Cleveland, or Philadelphia. The action became known as the Great Migration. America had never seen such a mass movement of its people. Chicago's black population doubled between 1910 and 1920. Detroit's increased six-fold.

Some Southern towns and villages lost most or all of their black population. Often these emigrants moved to the same place in the North. "You had Louisiana clubs, Mississippi clubs, Alabama clubs," recalled longtime Chicagoan Margaret Burroughs.[7]

The Big City

Coming into Chicago on the Illinois Central, first-time travelers experienced a whole new world. In the South, most knew of farms and small towns. Now they saw huge factories belching smoke from chimneys that were taller than church steeples. If the train arrived at night, hundreds of city lights greeted them as they arrived at the downtown station. New arrivals noticed other differences. "It was strange to pause before a crowded newsstand and buy a newspaper without having to wait for a white man to be served," commented author Richard Wright.[8]

Blacks had to adjust to an entirely different lifestyle. Steel mills and meat packinghouses, not farms, were the main Chicago employers. These jobs offered far higher wages than farmwork, but they were physically dangerous. On Southern farms, African Americans followed the sun, working from sunup to sundown. Northern employers judged a workday by the clock, not the sun. Southern farm employers made allowances for older or disabled workers. Northern factories were not so generous.

The *Defender* pictured a Northern land of opportunity. Chicago, for example, had jobs, schools, and better housing than the South. Nightclubs promised an active social life. Chicago even had the American Giants, the best black baseball team in the nation.

Those who came north expecting a paradise, however, found themselves disappointed. They suffered in the workplace. Blacks were often the last hired and the first fired. They were given the most menial and low-paying tasks. Most labor unions, which courted European immigrants, closed their doors to black workers.

Blacks found that segregation was not confined to the South. "It was understood that there were certain restaurants downtown where you couldn't eat," said Chicago journalist Vernon Jarrett. "Clubs . . . had black entertainers, but the management told them to discourage their friends from watching them perform."[9]

Many blacks preferred to live apart from white people. Many, if not most whites, also wanted such segregation.

Recent arrivals from the South often got little sympathy from established black residents. Many of these longtime settlers were prosperous. They resented the coarse language, rough manners, and questionable hygiene of the migrants. Some feared that the new neighbors would reflect badly on them with the white community.

Unofficial but very real boundaries separated the races. By law, Chicago beaches were integrated. In truth, there were "black" beaches and "white" ones. When some black swimmers accidentally drifted near a white beach in the summer of 1919, Chicago erupted in a massive race riot, which lasted more than two months. By the time the rioting stopped, at least fifteen whites and twenty-three blacks were dead. More than five hundred others were injured. It was a vivid reminder of the tensions the Great Migration was causing between whites and blacks as they competed for jobs, housing, and even recreation.

Even if the black migrants did not find paradise in the North, most could expect a better life than the one they left in the South. They could send their children to integrated schools. They received cash wages, which they could spend as they liked. If their employers displeased them, they could leave their jobs. They had opportunities beyond their wildest hopes. "I never even contemplated going into a public library in the South," claimed Vernon Jarrett.[10]

Most of all, the North offered the feeling that life could be better. Author Richard Wright explained, "The North symbolized to me all I had not felt and seen, it had no relation whatever to what actually existed. Yet by imagining a place where everything was possible, I kept hope alive in me."[11]

THE KEY TO INDEPENDENCE

African Americans knew that education was important. An educated person could make his or her own decisions. An educated farmer could total his own accounts at the end of the planting season without relying on the white foremen. Education was the key to independence, and an independent black population was the last thing Southern whites wanted.

Education

Black education was virtually nonexistent in the South before the Civil War. Most African Americans were slaves. White masters felt slaves needed to know only how to do their jobs. Blacks learned survival skills: how to act humble, how to hide their real feelings when insulted, how to soothe the egos of white people.

Access to free public education was unknown until after the war. At that time, the Freedmen's Bureau opened schools for blacks. More than four thousand such public schools appeared. Even after the bureau disbanded in 1872, many schools survived.

Blacks got their education wherever they could. Any available building might serve as a black school.

Most schools lacked supplies such as books, pencils, blackboards, and maps. Schools were frequently overcrowded. Black teachers earned a fraction of what their white colleagues received. States often used funds aimed for black education in white schools. Thus, blacks were being taxed to educate whites.

Black children had shorter school years than white kids. Blacks usually did not start classes until the end of the cotton harvesting season. This could be any time from November to January. Classes ended in early spring, at the start of the planting season.

"The Right and Power of a State"

Educational inequalities existed, but not everyone was willing to accept them without a struggle. In most cases, courts sided with the white-controlled government, even when injustice was obvious.

One such case involved schools in Richmond, Virginia. The city had separate schools for white male, white female, and black students. When the black grammar school became overcrowded, school officials closed the black high school and moved the black elementary students there. All white schools remained open.

Black plaintiffs claimed that the white high schools should be closed as well. The case went to the Supreme Court. Its justices ruled that the states, not the federal government, should control education. The black plaintiffs lost the case.

A 1908 case involved a small college in eastern Kentucky. Berea College was a private Christian school that did not receive state funds. Nevertheless, the Kentucky government ruled that it had broken state laws by admitting both black and white students. Kentucky law said a college could admit both black and white students—if their classes were at least twenty-five miles from each other.

The college protested. The college claimed that, by denying students the right to study together, the government was denying freedom of religion. The Supreme Court did not agree. Because the college was incorporated in Kentucky, it had to obey Kentucky laws.

African Americans were not the only victims of educational discrimination. A Chinese-American girl named Martha Lin tried to enter an all-white school in Mississippi. Her father was not fighting segregation; he just wanted the best possible education for his daughter. This case, too, failed in the United States Supreme Court. Chief Justice William Howard Taft wrote, "The right and power of a state to regulate the method of providing for the education of its youth at public expense is clear."[1]

Progress in destroying Jim Crow education ranged from slow to nonexistent. Even African-American educator W.E.B. Du Bois suggested that blacks were better off improving black schools than trying to desegregate all-white ones.

Social Engineers

Charles Houston, along with two hundred thousand other African Americans, volunteered for military service in World War I. College-educated Houston soon became an officer. His rank, however, did not mean he got respect from his white fellow soldiers. Poor treatment from whites made him determined to fight for racial justice.

In 1929, Houston became dean of the Howard University Law School. He took the lightly regarded law school and soon made it respected. Houston once claimed, "a lawyer is either a social engineer or a parasite to society."[2] He gathered some of the finest young black legal minds in the country, including a Baltimore native named Thurgood Marshall.

Houston joined the National Association for the Advancement of Colored People (NAACP) legal staff in 1934. Five years later, he started the NAACP Legal Defense Fund. The fund's primary mission was "to render free legal aid to Negroes who suffer legal injustice because of their race or color and cannot afford to employ legal assistance."[3] At first, the defense fund's staff consisted of Thurgood Marshall and a clerk. It would soon record an impressive number of victories.

Marshall's strategy was to start with cases with the best chance of victory in the courts. He would use these wins as precedents to argue in later cases. Marshall looked for cases in the border Southern states. He felt whites in those states were less hardened about segregation than in Deep South states such as

Mississippi and Alabama. He went after cases involving unequal pay for teachers. If school districts were forced to pay black teachers as much as whites, the added costs might encourage the districts to end segregation. He wanted cases involving college students, because whites might be less opposed to integration in colleges than in elementary schools.

Marshall scored his first major victory in his native Maryland. Donald Murray, an African American, was denied admission to the University of Maryland's law school because of his race. In 1936, the Supreme Court ordered the law school to admit Murray. Soon after, Marshall sued a Maryland school district that was paying black teachers less than whites.

Herman Sweatt, a mail carrier, sought admission to the University of Texas law school. The university refused. In 1948, the Supreme Court ruled that black applicants must be admitted to law schools reserved for whites unless equivalent facilities were available to them.

Texas hastily created a separate law school for blacks. But as had happened many times before, separate was not equal. The all-white University of Texas law school was considered one of the best in the nation. Its black counterpart, the Texas Law School for Negroes, hardly measured up. It started with four basement rooms, two professors, and no law library. On June 5, 1950, the Supreme Court decided *Sweatt* v. *Painter* in the plaintiff's favor. The formerly all-white

University of Texas Law School had to admit black students.

The man largely responsible for victories such as Sweatt's did not live to see Sweatt triumph. Charles Houston died on April 22, 1950. The decision in Sweatt's favor would not have surprised him. Before he died, Houston predicted "there come times when it is possible to forecast results of a contest, of a battle, of a lawsuit long before the final event has taken place. And so far as the struggle for civil rights is concerned, the struggle is won."[4]

Brown v. Board of Education

Although Kansas had remained loyal to the Union during the Civil War, segregation existed there, even in the capital of Topeka. Linda Brown was a victim of the segregation. She lived five blocks away from an all-white school. But she had to walk through a railroad yard, catch a school bus, and ride twenty-one blocks to her all-black school. Even though the schools were roughly equal in quality, Brown's father, Oliver, felt Linda was denied the right to the best possible education.

Topeka officials said the city was authorized to have segregated schools. In truth, the law declared that cities with more than fifteen thousand people could (but did not have to) segregate their schools. If Linda Brown was kept from a nearby school, it was the local school board and not the state that was responsible.

Brown et al. v. *Board of Education of Topeka, Shawnee Co., Kansas, et al.* began hearings on June 25, 1951. A month later, the school board passed a resolution to end segregation "as soon as possible."[5] The plaintiffs and their NAACP backers refused to accept this promise. They took the case to the United States Supreme Court.

Four other cases also came before the court, two from Delaware and one each from Virginia and South Carolina. The Court decided to lump all these cases together with *Brown* as one lawsuit. Since it had agreed to take the *Brown* case first, the five cases became known as *Brown* v. *Board of Education*. A similar case dealt with segregation in Washington, D.C., schools. Because the District of Columbia was a federally run district and not a state, *Bolling* v. *Sharpe* would be decided separately from the other cases.

Lawyers argued the cases before the Supreme Court in December 1952. There were ten one-hour presentations: five by the plaintiffs in the five state cases, and five by the defending school boards. Then all sides went home, hoping for quick decisions.

Those decisions did not come quickly. Supreme Court members appeared to be divided on the verdict. If they acted immediately, they would have a split decision. Justice Felix Frankfurter suggested rehearing the cases in December 1953. His colleagues agreed.

Fred Vinson, the chief justice, said that he did not wish to reverse the *Plessy* ruling. Southerners Tom Clark and Stanley Reed appeared ready to follow

Vinson. So did Justices Harold Burton and Sherman Minton. Frankfurter and Robert Jackson were unpredictable. Only William Douglas and ex–Klan member Hugo Black appeared to favor desegregation.

Chief Justice Vinson died suddenly in the summer of 1953. With his passing, the whole tone of the case changed.

The Warren Court and the *Brown* Decision

After Vinson's death, President Dwight Eisenhower had to nominate a new Supreme Court chief justice. He chose Earl Warren, who had been a popular California governor.

Warren's nomination worried several people. As a state official in California during World War II, Warren had favored the forced removal of one hundred thousand Japanese Americans from the state. (During the war, many people were afraid that Japanese Americans were working for Japan, the United States' enemy. In some places, Japanese Americans were forced to leave the country or were held in internment camps until the war was over.) People wondered whether Warren would ignore people's rights similarly in Supreme Court cases. One of Warren's early actions seemed to show that he no longer favored discrimination. When Warren arrived at the Supreme Court in 1953, the Court had separate washrooms for whites and blacks. Warren immediately desegregated the washrooms.

Attorneys presented their cases again in *Brown* in late 1953. Warren realized that *Brown* v. *Board of Education* would be one of the most important decisions in American history. He wanted the vote to be unanimous.

The 1950s, after the end of World War II, was a strange time in American politics. Now that the United States was facing off with its Cold War opponent, the Communist Soviet Union, appearances were important. For years, the Soviets and other governments around the world had used the racial tension and violence in the United States as part of their argument that the United States was inferior to other nations. It was especially important to many American politicians at the time of the *Brown* case for the United States to look as if it were making progress in improving racial relations.

Gradually, Chief Justice Warren won over reluctant justices.

Little Rock

On May 12, 1954, the Supreme Court gave its unanimous decision. It struck down the notion of separate but equal in the field of education. But making the decision was only the first part of dismantling inequalities that had existed for centuries. How would the integration of schools be enforced?

One thing was certain: The judges would not oversee desegregation themselves. School districts would handle desegregation individually.

In 1955, the Supreme Court made its second announcement on the *Brown* case. This decision,

THE OPINIONS OF THAT DATE [MAY 17, 1954—THE ORIGINAL *BROWN* DECISION], DECLARING THE FUNDAMENTAL PRINCIPLE THAT RACIAL DISCRIMINATION IN PUBLIC EDUCATION IS UNCONSTITUTIONAL, ARE INCORPORATED HEREIN BY REFERENCE. . . .

AT STAKE IS THE PERSONAL INTEREST OF THE PLAINTIFFS IN ADMISSION TO PUBLIC SCHOOLS AS SOON AS PRACTICABLE ON A NONDISCRIMINATORY BASIS. TO EFFECTUATE THIS INTEREST MAY CALL FOR ELIMINATION OF A VARIETY OF OBSTACLES IN MAKING THE TRANSITION TO SCHOOL SYSTEMS OPERATED IN ACCORDANCE WITH THE CONSTITUTIONAL PRINCIPLES SET FORTH IN OUR MAY 17, 1954, DECISION. COURTS OF EQUITY MAY PROPERLY TAKE INTO ACCOUNT THE PUBLIC INTEREST IN THE ELIMINATION OF SUCH OBSTACLES IN A SYSTEMATIC AND EFFECTIVE MANNER. BUT IT SHOULD GO WITHOUT SAYING THAT THE VITALITY OF THESE CONSTITUTIONAL PRINCIPLES CANNOT BE ALLOWED TO YIELD SIMPLY BECAUSE OF DISAGREEMENT WITH THEM.[6]

In 1955, the Supreme Court issued a follow-up to its 1955 Brown *v.* Board of Education *decision, telling the states that schools should be integrated "with all deliberate speed."*

sometimes referred to as *Brown II*, called on districts to integrate their schools with "all deliberate speed."[7] This vague phrase produced varying results. Baltimore, Maryland; St. Louis, Missouri; Louisville, Kentucky; and Wilmington, Delaware; desegregated their schools within a year. Little Rock, Arkansas, desegregated, too—but only after an ugly episode that gripped the nation.

In Little Rock, "deliberate speed" meant waiting more than two years for formerly all-white schools to admit blacks. Even then, the integration was far from total. Only one school—working-class Central High School—would be integrated. And only nine black students would join the white students there.

Carlotta Walls, Jefferson Thomas, Elizabeth Eckford, Thilma Mothershed, Gloria Ray, Melba Patillo, Ernest Green, Terrance Roberts, and Minnijean Brown were chosen as the black students who would integrate Central High. They eagerly waited for school to start on September 3, 1957.

Many whites failed to share their enthusiasm. Some filed a petition in an Arkansas court to prevent desegregation. It appeared that the school opening would not proceed peacefully.

Orval Faubus had won election as Arkansas governor in 1954. By local standards, he had been a moderate. Many Southern politicians boasted about how they intended to keep segregation. At first, Faubus avoided such talk. He won re-election in 1956. But another election would come in 1958, and he knew what the most vocal voters wanted. Before the school year began, he declared that he would not force integration on the people of Arkansas, whom, he said, did not want it.

On August 29, Faubus appeared before a local court and issued an order forbidding desegregation. He declared that "blood will run in the streets" if blacks tried to enter Central High School.[8] A federal district court, however, ordered the desegregation to take place.

Instead, Governor Faubus ordered hundreds of Arkansas National Guard troops to keep the black students out of the school. When the students arrived, the troops turned them away.

Federal Judge Ronald Davies ordered Governor Faubus to allow the nine black students to enter the high school. Faubus refused. The Little Rock school board spoke to the governor on the students' behalf. Still, Faubus refused to help the blacks. Davies set September 20 as the date for a hearing on his order. The United States Department of Justice gave a report on the side of the students.

This was no small event that was taking place. Reporters from major newspapers covered the unsuccessful integration attempt. More important, television cameras brought the spectacle into living rooms across the country. Viewers in Los Angeles, New York, and Chicago saw American citizens being refused a basic right because of their race.

Among those aware of these events was President Dwight David Eisenhower. The president was not a firm civil rights supporter. However, Governor Faubus was disobeying a court order. As a former soldier, Eisenhower was a firm believer in following orders. Eisenhower met with Faubus on September 14 in Newport, Rhode Island. Faubus said he would keep the National Guard on duty, but would admit the black students to school. After the meeting, he went back on that promise. On September 20, Faubus ordered the National Guard removed from Central High School.

With the National Guard gone, the nine black students entered the high school through a side door. When the white mob discovered the students' presence, members began attacking the Little Rock police, who were guarding the building.

Eisenhower could not ignore this disturbance. He placed the Arkansas National Guard under federal control and ordered them back to Central High School. He also ordered the 101st Airborne Division from Fort Campbell, Kentucky, to Little Rock.

Surrounded by soldiers, the students could at last go to school in safety. One of them, Melba Patillo, recalled:

> As we neared the school, I could hear the roar of a helicopter directly overhead. Our convoy was joined by more jeeps. . . . Closer to the school, we saw more soldiers and many more hostile white people with scowls on their faces, lining the sidewalk and shaking their fists. But for the first time I wasn't afraid of them.[9]

A soldier stands guard in front of Little Rock's Central High School, the site of one of the most controversial integration attempts of the civil rights era.

The black students entered the school and stayed there all day without incident. By October 14, Eisenhower had ordered the removal of half of the federal troops. On October 23, students entered the school without military escorts. Eisenhower ordered the paratroopers removed in late November, although the National Guard stayed there for the rest of the school year. Although the black students endured continuous insults and humiliations, only one failed to stay for the entire school year.

Governor Faubus ordered Central High School closed for the 1958–1959 school year. White students went to private schools and blacks returned to all-black schools. In June 1959, a United States district court voided that plan. Central High School reopened in September, and black students entered without incident.

The end of the Little Rock crisis did not end all school segregation. Twelve years after the *Brown* decision, some school districts still had not let African Americans enter all-white schools. Mississippi and Alabama admitted black students to state universities only after President John F. Kennedy had called out National Guard troops. But Little Rock was a milestone. The federal government showed that it would use force if necessary to protect the educational rights of students, regardless of race.

8

"IF NOT US, WHO?"

Gradually, attitudes changed. For the most part, it was blacks, not whites, who led the change. In the 1950s and 1960s, African Americans throughout the South protested their conditions. Many whites fought any move toward reform. "They viewed that anything they gave us would be viewed as just a start," claimed Montgomery, Alabama, activist Jo Ann Robinson. "And you know, they were probably right."[1]

The Montgomery Bus Boycott

Rosa Parks was a slender, quiet, forty-two-year-old woman. She hardly seemed to be the material from which legends are made. But Rosa Parks was the right woman in the right place at the right time.

Rosa Parks probably did not feel like a hero on December 1, 1955. She worked as a seamstress at a downtown department store in Montgomery, Alabama. She altered clothing and ran a steam press. Parks had been on her feet all day. She was exhausted as she waited for her ride home on the Cleveland Avenue bus.

Throughout the 1950s and 1960s, African Americans and their supporters staged marches like this one to protest the continued segregation of public facilities.

Four fifths of Montgomery bus riders were blacks. However, the local bus company reserved the first ten rows of seats for whites. If whites filled their seats, blacks had to give up their own.

The Cleveland Avenue bus was crowded that Thursday afternoon. Soon, white passengers filled the first rows of seats. Parks and three other blacks were seated in the first row behind the white section. A white man wanted to sit down. Bus driver J. F. Blake ordered all the blacks in the first black row to leave their seats. Rosa Parks remained seated.

"When the driver saw me still sitting, he asked if I was going to stand up, and I said, 'No, I'm not,'" she said later. "And then he said, 'Well, if you don't stand up, I'm going to call the police and have you arrested.' I said, 'You may do that.'"[2]

An observer of the arrest called Edgar Nixon, the city's most notable black leader. Nixon had known Rosa Parks for years. He headed the local NAACP chapter, where Parks served as a volunteer secretary.

Parks's arrest might not have surprised Nixon. After all, black bus riders had complained for years of hassles by white drivers. When the person arrested was Rosa Parks, Nixon figured it was time for action. If the black community could rally around anyone, it was Rosa Parks. "She was decent," Nixon said. "She was committed. . . . You had to respect her as a lady. . . . [W]hen she did something, people just figured it was the right thing to do."[3]

SOURCE DOCUMENT

THE NEXT STOP WAS THE EMPIRE THEATER, AND SOME
WHITES GOT ON. THEY FILLED UP THE WHITE SEATS, AND
ONE MAN WAS LEFT STANDING. THE DRIVER . . . LOOKED
BACK AT US. HE SAID . . . "Y'ALL BETTER MAKE IT LIGHT ON
YOURSELVES AND LET ME HAVE THOSE SEATS." . . .

I THOUGHT BACK TO A TIME WHEN I USED TO SIT UP ALL
NIGHT AND DIDN'T SLEEP, AND MY GRANDFATHER WOULD
HAVE HIS GUN RIGHT BY THE FIREPLACE. . . . PEOPLE
ALWAYS SAY THAT I DIDN'T GIVE UP MY SEAT BECAUSE I WAS
TIRED, BUT THAT ISN'T TRUE. I WAS NOT TIRED PHYSICALLY,
OR NO MORE TIRED THAN I USUALLY WAS AT THE END OF A
WORKING DAY. I WAS NOT OLD, ALTHOUGH SOME PEOPLE
HAVE AN IMAGE OF ME AS BEING OLD THEN. I WAS FORTY-
TWO. NO, THE ONLY TIRED I WAS, WAS TIRED OF GIVING IN.[4]

*Rosa Parks, whose brave actions in defying the
segregation of Montgomery, Alabama buses, later gave
this account of her reasons for setting off one of the
largest civil rights protests in history.*

That night, Nixon discussed the case with Parks and her family. They decided to organize a one-day boycott of the Montgomery bus line. They called attorney Fred Gray, who then called Jo Ann Robinson. She met with three friends at Alabama State College. The four of them spent most of the night producing thirty-five thousand leaflets to be distributed throughout Montgomery's black neighborhoods. The leaflets asked all blacks not to ride city buses on Monday, December 5.

Transportation boycotts by blacks were nothing new in the South. Ever since the 1880s, African Americans who resented white treatment had tried protests. However, they lacked alternative forms of transportation. Most boycotts lasted a few weeks at most, then fizzled. This time, conditions were different. Many black Montgomery residents had cars, taxis, or other means of travel. They also had organization, which was lacking in previous generations.

More than a hundred black leaders met at Dexter Avenue Baptist Church on Friday, December 2. They looked at the boycott not as a one-day event, but as a possible long-term war. They asked black taxi drivers to give free or low-cost rides. They mapped out routes and determined drop-off and pick-up points for passengers.

Boycott leaders spent the weekend contacting almost every black resident in the city. Montgomery's black ministers agreed to speak to their congregations on Sunday morning. Some ministers toured the city's bars and nightclubs on Saturday night, talking to those who might not be churchgoers.

The Reverend Martin Luther King, Jr., the young minister of Dexter Avenue Baptist Church, looked out his window early Monday morning. The normally crowded bus was empty. That scene repeated itself throughout the city. Black residents of Montgomery were staying off the buses.

Meanwhile, Rosa Parks went to the city court. She paid a fourteen-dollar fine but appealed the case. More than five hundred of her supporters accompanied her.

Boycott leaders called for a meeting that evening at Holt Street Baptist Church. Thousands attended. Ministers and congregations agreed that the boycott must continue. At this meeting, they organized the Montgomery Improvement Association (MIA). Martin Luther King, Jr., was chosen as the new group's leader.

Mayor W. A. Gayle did not appear to be worried after the boycott's first day. He predicted, "Comes the first rainy day and the Negroes will be back on the buses."[5]

"A Stick-togetherness"

Rainy days passed. Cold days passed. Instead of wearying of the boycott, black protesters became stronger. "There was a stick-togetherness that drew them like a magnet," Jo Ann Robinson recalled.[6]

The boycott was remarkably successful. The bus company had lost so many riders that it asked for permission to double its fares. More than the bus line suffered. The boycott began in December, the busiest shopping month of the year. Many blacks who boycotted the buses also stayed away from downtown, white-owned stores. Those stores made $2 million less than during the previous holiday season.

Some wealthy whites indirectly supported the protest by transporting their maids or domestic workers, who refused to take the bus.

Some whites fought back. Rosa Parks and her husband lost their jobs. The city ordered taxis to stop giving free rides. This kept most boycotters from taking the cabs. When cars started carrying people to and from work for a fifteen-cent gas fee, police stopped the drivers of those cars and arrested them for operating a taxi without a license.

The MIA responded by organizing a volunteer car pool. Cars picked up riders without charging a fee. The MIA paid gasoline and mechanical expenses. Churches bought several cars with MIA funds and used them exclusively for the boycott. Volunteer dispatchers sent cars where they were needed. Each day, 325 cars picked up riders at 48 dispatch points. Even the Montgomery police department admired the operation.

The boycott cost money. The MIA spent about $4,000 per week. It got money from church collections and bake sales. As news of the boycott's success spread, donations came in from around the country.

In January 1956, city commissioners announced that the city council had reached a settlement with a group of black ministers. King contacted the ministers who had met the whites. They denied any settlement. When word of this phony agreement reached the black community, blacks became more suspicious of whites than ever.

On January 26, Martin Luther King, Jr., was arrested for driving thirty miles per hour in a twenty-five-mile-per-hour zone. He was taken to the police station and fingerprinted, then released. A few days later, a white extremist bombed the minister's house. Within minutes, more than five hundred people gathered at King's home. When police ordered them to leave, they would not do so. They left only when asked by King.

The bombing made blacks more determined than ever. On January 31, attorney Fred Gray filed a lawsuit to outlaw segregation on the Montgomery bus system. White Montgomery residents also went to the courts. On February 21, a special grand jury indicted 115 of the boycott's leaders, including Nixon and Rosa Parks. King, however, was the real target. He was the only one who went to trial. King was found guilty. He faced a five-hundred-dollar fine or 386 days of hard labor.

This was terrible publicity for Montgomery's white community. Already the local government, police department, and newspapers were being ridiculed by the national media. Now protest leader King was viewed as a martyr, and the white establishment as a group of bullies.

Meanwhile, federal courts sided with the boycotters. On June 4, a three-judge panel ruled Montgomery's bus segregation unconstitutional. The city appealed. But in November, the Supreme Court upheld the panel's ruling. The Court's order was officially served in Montgomery on December 20, 1956.

The year-long animosity seemed to melt immediately. The following morning at 5:45 A.M., King, Nixon, Gray, Abernathy, and Parks waited at a bus stop outside King's home. The driver smiled and said, "I believe you are Reverend King, aren't you?"

"Yes, I am," King answered.

"We are glad to have you this morning," the driver told him.[7]

Sit-ins

The F. W. Woolworth store in Greensboro, North Carolina, irritated Ralph Johns. He hated the fact that black customers were not served at the store's lunch counter. Woolworth's was not unique. Lunch counters were a part of many department stores. In almost all cases in the South, blacks could shop in the stores but could not eat there.

Johns, a clothing salesman and former movie actor, felt a protest was necessary. As a white man, he was not the appropriate person to lead such an action. Johns sought blacks whose desire for action outweighed their fear of consequences. Greensboro's black college, North Carolina A & T, had several such students. In fact, the school had a reputation for activism.

Johns approached freshman Joseph McNeil just before Thanksgiving in 1959. "I says, 'Joe, you got any guts?' . . ." he recalled.[8] Johns explained his plan for black students to sit at the Woolworth's lunch counter until they were served. McNeil said he would think about it.

McNeil took no action until after Christmas vacation. When he returned to school, an arrogant waitress brushed crumbs on him and refused him service. McNeil returned to Johns and plotted action.

In early February 1960, four black students entered Woolworth's and made small purchases. When one student requested something to eat at the lunch counter, the waitress told him that the store did not serve blacks. He pulled out a receipt and said, "You just finished serving me at a counter two feet from here."[9] The waitress still refused to serve him. The store's manager did nothing. All four students remained until closing time.

The next day, they brought company. When the students were refused service, they remained at the counter and read books. Day after day, the number of protesters at these "sit-ins" grew. The idea spread to other stores in Greensboro and across the South. Some stores retaliated by closing their lunch counters.

City officials agreed to negotiate the dispute. Students agreed to call off the sit-ins during negotiations. But the city kept delaying. By the first of April, many students felt they were the victims of an April Fool's prank. They returned to the lunch counters.

Through the use of sit-ins, in which African Americans would sit in segregated places until they were served, African Americans were eventually able to enjoy the same public facilities, such as this lunch counter, as whites.

By the middle of summer, Woolworth's yielded. The store allowed blacks to be served at its lunch counters. Other stores grudgingly made the same decision. The success of the sit-ins led to read-ins at libraries, wade-ins at beaches, and kneel-ins at all-white churches.

Johns returned to the background, but not before receiving a notable visitor. The Reverend Martin Luther King, Jr., came to him and said, "Mr. Johns, I want you to know that someday our people will know what you have done, and they will thank you for it."[10]

Freedom Riders

Congress could pass laws to protect the rights of American citizens. But was anyone paying attention to those laws? In early 1961, a courageous group of activists decided to find out.

James Farmer, the director of the Congress of Racial Equality (CORE), said, "We knew we had to get the support of the country behind us to end segregation. We had to have some kind of dramatic project to attract the attention of the press, and especially television."[11] That project turned out to be an interracial bus trip that became known as the Freedom Ride.

The Freedom Riders set out in two buses from Washington, D.C., on May 4, 1961. They planned to stop in several Southern cities before arriving in New Orleans, Louisiana. At each stop, they would compare washroom and food facilities available for blacks and whites. The riders documented many racial inequalities along their way.

Neither bus would make it to New Orleans. Federal authorities did little to help the riders. The Federal Bureau of Investigation (FBI) had informants who warned of violence in Alabama. Yet the FBI did nothing to block such violence.

A mob of about two hundred people awaited the riders when they stopped at the northeastern Alabama town of Anniston. Members of the mob started beating on one bus and smashing in the windows. Demonstrating a point for civil rights would have to wait for another time. The bus and its passengers hurried out of town without stopping.

Five miles outside of town, the Freedom Riders' bus stopped. Its tires had been slashed by angry whites. The mob followed the bus to its stopping point. At first, riders locked themselves inside the bus. Then someone threw a firebomb inside.

Ironically, the bomb saved the Freedom Riders. It caused an explosion of the bus's gas tank, which scattered many of the attackers. Even so, others moved forward to attack the Freedom Riders. E. L. Cowling, an undercover official of the Alabama State Police, had been riding on the bus. At the last moment, he pulled out a gun and pointed it at the members of the white mob. He was able to hold them off until an ambulance could bring the riders to safety. The riders regrouped in Birmingham, Alabama, where they decided to abandon their mission.

The failure of one mission, however, did not mean the end of all missions. Another group of Freedom

Riders came from Nashville, Tennessee, to Birmingham. It met with violence in Montgomery. Despite the setbacks, a sense of victory prevailed. One of the riders, John Lewis, said "If not us, who? If not now, then when? . . . Will someone else's children have to risk their lives instead of us risking ours?"[12]

THE RIGHT TO SERVE, THE RIGHT TO VOTE

Like whites, African Americans paid taxes. Yet those taxes did not give them equal political representation. They were deprived of two important parts of the American experience—the right to equality in the military and the right to vote.

African Americans in the Military

Few sights angered a white Southerner more than a black man in a military uniform. First, the uniform meant honor—a quality whites hated to see in blacks. Second, soldiers carried weapons, and whites dreaded the thought of an armed black person.

After the Civil War, new military units formed from state militias. Black Southerners, barred from the militias, were kept out of the military. From the time of the Civil War, Congress had allowed black soldiers, but only in all-black regiments. Wherever they fought, black soldiers distinguished themselves. Colonel Theodore Roosevelt led a famous charge up San Juan Hill in Cuba during the Spanish-American War. Two black cavalry troops took part in the charge. By the end of the war, more than a hundred black soldiers were named officers.

During World War I, the all-black 369th Infantry Division performed with amazing valor. Its troops never lost ground, and never had a man captured. Another all-black unit, the 371st Infantry, also saw action in France. The grateful French government gave three officers the Legion of Honor and awarded the *Croix de Guerre* to thirty-four officers and eighty-nine enlisted men.

Yet bravery in combat did not bring blacks respect at home. Black soldiers, generally supervised by white officers, remained second-class citizens. Southern military bases, where most black troops did their training, rigidly enforced Jim Crow laws.

On the eve of World War II, the American military still kept races apart. A policy statement from Assistant Secretary of War Robert P. Patterson declared, "The policy of the War Department is not to intermingle colored and white enlisted personnel in the same regimental organizations. This policy has proved satisfactory over a long period of years."[1]

Although still segregated, black troops fought valiantly during World War II. The 99th Squadron, which trained at Tuskegee Institute, won impressive victories in Italy. This group, known as the Tuskegee Airmen, was one of the most celebrated American units in the war.

President Harry Truman appreciated the heroism of African Americans. He submitted a proposal to Congress in early 1948, calling for an end to discrimination and segregation in the armed forces. Southern Congress members opposed the bill. On July 26, Truman issued Executive Order 9981. It called for equality of treatment in the military. Black soldiers and sailors were now given equal rights by the president, their Commander in Chief. Many, however, would wait half a generation before they could vote for that commander.

The Right to Vote

Newly freed slaves had won the right to vote in 1870, thanks to the Fifteenth Amendment to the Constitution. That right proved short-lived. At first, terrorism and violence kept blacks from the polls. Later, state laws produced the same results.

Mississippi changed its constitution in 1890. The new document required voters to read or provide "a reasonable interpretation" of parts of the state constitution.[2] What was a "reasonable interpretation"? In reality, if a white man gave an interpretation, it was reasonable. If a black man said the same thing, it was most likely not.

Other states followed Mississippi's example. Soon, all Southern state constitutions had poll taxes or literacy test clauses. Some influential Southern blacks were given a pass to register and vote.

". . . More Negroes in Jail"

As late as 1960, many blacks in the South appeared as unlikely as their grandfathers to gain suffrage (the right to vote). But conditions were different later in the decade. Blacks had experienced struggles, and they had seen victories. Thanks to the *Brown* v. *Board of Education* decision, their children could go to school with white children. Thanks to the boycott in Montgomery, blacks could ride buses alongside whites. If blacks could be alongside whites at school or on a bus, why not at the ballot box?

White resistance was the reason why not. Martin Luther King, Jr., after a 1963 arrest for civil disobedience, gave a frightening commentary. "This is Selma, Alabama," he wrote. "There are more Negroes in jail with me than there are on the voting rolls."[3]

Selma

By the mid-1960s, Alabama had a reputation as one of the most repressive states toward blacks. Even by Alabama standards, the town of Selma was severe. Judge James Hare, the town's political leader, took the civil rights movement as a personal insult. In 1964, he issued an order to stop civil rights demonstrations in the town.

Hare's political ally, Sheriff Jim Clark, enforced Hare's orders. Thanks to television news coverage, many Americans stereotyped Southern sheriffs as bullying, bigoted brutes. Clark fit that image perfectly. When fifty would-be black voters came to register in late 1964, Clark and his deputies met them with electric cattle prods. Despite threats, black Selma residents and some white supporters continued to push for civil rights.

In February, demonstrators marched to the courthouse in nearby Marion. One of the marchers was Selma resident Jamie Lee Jackson. As the marchers neared the courthouse, troopers blocked their path. One chased Jackson into a nearby cafe. Jackson was shot while trying to protect his mother from troopers. He died a few days later.

Selma's voting rights movement now had a martyr. The Reverend James Bevel suggested more dramatic action. "I've got something to say to the governor about Jamie Lee Jackson," Bevel said. "I thought I would walk to Montgomery and tell the governor in person. Mr. Cage [Jackson's grandfather] has said he's willing to walk with me."[4] Bevel, Cage, and more than six hundred others prepared for a march from Selma to Montgomery on March 7, 1965.

Sheriff Clark had different ideas. Knowing the marchers would have to cross the Edmund Pettus Bridge over the Alabama River, Clark deputized most white men over the age of twenty-one to meet them. When the marchers tried to cross the bridge, whites attacked them with baseball bats, clubs, and tear gas. The thwarted march became known as Bloody Sunday.

White segregationists won the battle. But they were losing the war. Television cameras captured the violent event. Among those watching were ministers around the nation.

Martin Luther King, Jr., invited them for another march. On March 9, several hundred clergymen crossed the Pettus Bridge in a symbolic gesture. When the troopers met them, they returned to Selma. That night, white segregationists attacked one of the ministers. Reverend Jesse Reeb died two days later.

Meanwhile, a confrontation was taking place in the courtroom. Demonstrators, seeking to overrule the

The Selma to Montgomery march, organized by Martin Luther King, Jr., was one of the largest demonstrations for civil rights in Alabama, one of the most repressive of the Southern states.

order against demonstrations, appeared before federal Judge Frank Johnson. They showed him television footage of Bloody Sunday. John Lewis, one of those who was beaten, testified.

President Lyndon Johnson made a nationwide television address on March 11. He claimed it was "wrong—deadly wrong" to deny American citizens their voting rights.[5] The speech brought results. On March 20, Judge Johnson overturned Hare's injunction. President Johnson sent seventy deputy marshals to join Alabama National Guard members in protecting the marchers.

Once again, on March 21, the demonstrators proceeded. This time, the marchers numbered in the thousands. Whites took shots at them along their four-day journey. But more than thirty thousand people, black and white, joined in for the last three miles of the fifty-four-mile trek.

J im Crow was finally dying. Alabama Governor George Wallace in 1963 declared, "Segregation now, segregation tomorrow, and segregation forever."[1] But those who favored segregation were fighting a losing battle. The courts were against them. Thanks to the nationwide exposure of television, public opinion was against them. Some white Southerners fought back with the only weapon they had left—violence.

★ ★ ★
★ **10** ★
★ ★
★ ★ ★

VIOLENCE AND VICTORY

Emmett Till

It was supposed to be a relaxing summer vacation. Fourteen-year-old Emmett Till and his cousin, Curtis Jones, went from Chicago to rural Mississippi in 1955. Before Till left, his mother warned him to be careful, because customs were different in the South.

One day, Till and his cousin went to a grocery store. The owner's wife was tending the store by herself. It is not certain what Till did, but the woman considered it an improper advance. When her husband found out, he and his brother went to Curtis Jones's

Governor George Wallace (left) refused to integrate the University of Alabama, despite court orders to do so.

great-uncle's house and demanded "the boy from Chicago."[2] They took Till away and killed him. Three days later, his mutilated body was found.

Emmett Till's body was shipped back to Chicago. His mother demanded an open casket funeral, so that others could see the brutality of his murder. Black newspapers made this a front-page story for weeks. One civil rights leader commented, "There'd been killings like this for centuries, but times were changing. This was big news. Even in foreign countries, people wanted to know why a black boy had been murdered just for being fresh."[3]

The accused killers went to trial that September. It took an all-white jury little more than an hour to acquit them. Although both men were acquitted, the community never really forgave them for the disgrace they had caused. Both eventually moved away.

Other Violence

They called it "Freedom Summer." Whites and blacks from the North went to the South in 1964 to help blacks register to vote. Mississippi, which had a reputation as the most racist state in the Union, was a particular target.

New Yorkers Michael Schwerner and Andrew Goodman went to Meridian, Mississippi. There, they joined James Chaney, a black civil rights worker. On June 21, they left for Philadelphia, in Neshoba County. Ku Klux Klan members had burned a church there the

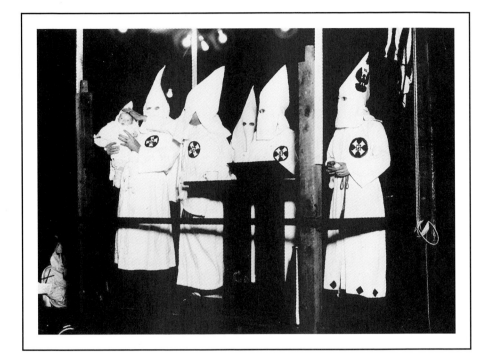

Members of racist organizations such as the Ku Klux Klan became violent in their efforts to stop the progress African Americans were making through the civil rights movement.

week before. All three knew the risks involved. Schwerner warned, "One must keep in mind that Neshoba is very 'tough' country."[4]

When they reached Philadelphia at about 3:00 P.M., a deputy sheriff stopped and hassled them. Seven hours later, the three were released. Another deputy sheriff stopped them about ten miles outside of town and turned them over to a white mob. They were never seen alive again.

An informer tipped off the FBI about the killings. A month after they were reported missing, the bodies of Goodman, Chaney, and Schwerner were found underneath a makeshift dam. The killers were brought to trial. The Supreme Court upheld their convictions in 1970.

Even top-ranking civil rights leaders faced extreme danger every day. Medgar Evers was the NAACP field secretary for Mississippi in 1963. Historian David Halberstam called Evers "perhaps the bravest man in America."[5] As he was returning home on the night of June 12, a sniper shot him. He died almost instantly. Even though Byron Beckwith bragged of having killed Evers, a jury at first acquitted him. He was not convicted until more than thirty years later.

"I would like to live a long life . . . but I'm not concerned about that now," said Martin Luther King, Jr., at a rally for striking Memphis sanitation workers on April 3, 1968. "I've seen the promised land. I may not get there with you. . . ."[6] Seldom have words been more prophetic. King was shot to death the following

I HAVE A DREAM THAT ONE DAY THIS NATION WILL RISE UP AND LIVE OUT THE TRUE MEANING OF ITS CREED—"WE HOLD THESE TRUTHS TO BE SELF-EVIDENT: THAT ALL MEN ARE CREATED EQUAL."

I HAVE A DREAM THAT ONE DAY ON THE RED HILLS OF GEORGIA THE SONS OF FORMER SLAVES AND THE SONS OF FORMER SLAVEOWNERS WILL BE ABLE TO SIT DOWN TOGETHER AT A TABLE OF BROTHERHOOD. . . .

I HAVE A DREAM THAT MY FOUR CHILDREN WILL ONE DAY LIVE IN A NATION WHERE THEY WILL NOT BE JUDGED BY THE COLOR OF THEIR SKIN BUT BY THE CONTENT OF THEIR CHARACTER.

I HAVE A DREAM TODAY.[7]

Martin Luther King's famous "I Have a Dream" speech became one of the most memorable statements in support of the civil rights movement.

evening. His assassination set off riots in cities throughout the United States.

" . . . the Promised Land"

Violence did not lead to long-term gains for those who favored segregation. If anything, reaction against the violence helped blacks and whites who favored integration.

Two constitutional amendments helped secure black voting rights. The Twenty-third Amendment, adopted in 1961, allowed residents of the mostly black District of Columbia to vote in presidential elections. Three years later, the Twenty-fourth Amendment became part of the Constitution. It forbade states from requiring poll taxes for presidential elections. President Lyndon Johnson called the amendment "a triumph of liberty over restriction."[8] In 1964, a sweeping civil rights law outlawed segregation and discrimination in jobs, public accommodations, education, and voting. It also created the Equal Employment Opportunity Commission (EEOC).

Activists Jamie Lee Jackson, James Reeb, and others did not die in vain. Five months after the Selma demonstrations in 1965, President Lyndon Johnson signed a voting rights act. This law suspended literacy tests in Southern states where fewer than 50 percent of adults had voted the year before. It also provided federal supervision of elections, to assure that African Americans were not kept from the polls.

Martin Luther King, Jr., who was assassinated in 1968, remains a hero of the civil rights movement, which finally succeeded in bringing the Jim Crow era to an end.

Another civil rights bill was passed shortly after King's death in 1968. This one prevented discrimination in the sale or rental of most housing.

"We as a people will get to the promised land," Martin Luther King proclaimed just before he was assassinated.[9] If he meant total equality in education or employment opportunities, that promised land has still not been reached. But at long last, the Jim Crow era is over, and all Americans—white, black, or any other race—are considered equal in the eyes of the law.

★ TIMELINE ★

1865—Former slaves are freed at end of Civil War.

1865 –1866—Southern states enact Black Codes, repressive laws against African Americans.

1867—Congress passes the Reconstruction Act.

1868—All citizens are given equal rights under newly ratified Fourteenth Amendment.

1870—Mississippi's Hiram Revels becomes the first black United States senator.

1875—A major civil rights act forbids discrimination in public accommodations.

1877—A specially appointed panel gives Republican Rutherford B. Hayes the votes needed to become president; After taking office, Hayes removes troops from the South, ending Reconstruction.

1883—Supreme Court rules the 1875 Civil Rights Act unconstitutional.

1895—Booker T. Washington's "Cast down your bucket" speech helps make him the most powerful African American in the country.

1896—*Plessy* v. *Ferguson* Supreme Court verdict establishes the "separate but equal" doctrine.

1905—W.E.B. Du Bois organizes the Niagara Movement, which calls for an end to segregation.

1909—A New York City conference establishes the National Association for the Advancement of Colored People (NAACP).

1915—Hit film *Birth of a Nation* sparks a revival of the Ku Klux Klan.

1916 –1919—Half a million Southern blacks go north in a movement called the Great Migration.

1954—*Brown* v. *Board of Education* verdict forbids segregation in public schools.

1955 –1956—Black residents of Montgomery, Alabama, stage a massive bus boycott.

1957—Black students, guarded by federal troops, integrate Little Rock's Central High School.

1960—Students in Greensboro, North Carolina, begin the first of a series of "sit-ins."

1961—Freedom Riders escape after violence in Alabama cities.

1963—Martin Luther King, Jr., delivers his famous "I have a dream" speech before a huge civil rights demonstration in Washington, D.C.

1964—Twenty-fourth Amendment outlaws poll taxes in federal elections; A sweeping civil rights bill makes discrimination in public accommodations illegal.

1965—Voting Rights Act permits federal supervision of Southern elections.

1968—Fair Housing Act prevents discrimination in sale or rental of most housing; Martin Luther King, Jr., is assassinated.

★ CHAPTER NOTES ★

Chapter 1. "The Most Important Decision"

1. Leonard A. Stevens, *Equal! The Case of Integration vs. Jim Crow* (New York: Coward, McCann, and Geohagen, 1976), p. 130.

2. David Halberstam, *The Fifties* (New York: Fawcett Columbine, 1993), p. 414.

3. Bernard Schwartz, *A History of the Supreme Court* (New York: Oxford University, 1993), pp. 305–306.

4. Ibid.

5. Halberstam, p. 424.

6. Schwartz, p. 307.

7. Stevens, p. 131.

8. Geoffrey R. Stone, Louis M. Sedman, Cass R. Sunstein, and Mark V. Tushnet, *Constitutional Law,* 2nd ed. (Boston: Little, Brown, and Company, 1991), pp. 497, 498, 499.

9. Clayborne Carson et al., eds., *The Eyes on the Prize Civil Rights Reader* (New York: Viking Penguin, 1991), p. 36.

Chapter 2. Less-Than-Free Freedmen

1. Berman E. Johnson, *The Dream Deferred: A Survey of Black America 1840–1896* (Dubuque, Iowa: Kendall/Hunt, 1993), p. 88.

2. Henry Steele Commager, ed., *Documents of American History,* 6th ed. (New York: Appleton-Century-Crofts, Inc. 1958), vol. 2, p. 14.

3. Claude G. Bowers, *The Tragic Era: The Revolution After Lincoln* (Cambridge, Mass.: Houghton Mifflin, 1929), p. 309.

4. Eric Foner, *Reconstruction: America's Unfinished Revolution* (New York: Harper and Row, 1988), p. 342.

5. Ibid., p. 429.

6. Ibid., p. 427.

7. Kenneth M. Stampp, *The Era of Reconstruction, 1865–1877* (New York: Vintage Books, 1965), p. 4.

8. William J. Ridings, Jr., and Stewart B. McIver, *Rating the Presidents: A Ranking of U.S. Leaders, from the Great and Honorable to the Dishonest and Incompetent* (New York: Citadel, 1997), p. 130.

9. Bernard Schwartz, *A History of the Supreme Court* (New York: Oxford, 1993), p. 167.

10. Leonard A. Stevens, *Equal! The Case of Integration vs. Jim Crow* (New York: Coward, McCann, and Geohagen, 1976), p. 37.

Chapter 3. Life Under Jim Crow

1. Marion Figgs, producer/director, *Ethnic Notions: Black People in White Minds* (California Newsreel, 1987).

2. *Take Me to Chicago The Promised Land* (Discovery, British Broadcasting Corporation, 1989).

3. W.E.B. Du Bois, *Souls of Black Folk*, quoted in Leon F. Litwack, *Trouble in Mind: Black Southerners in the Age of Jim Crow* (New York: Alfred A. Knopf, 1998), p. 240.

4. Pauli Murray, *Proud Shoes: The Story of an American Family*, quoted in Litwack, *Trouble in Mind*, p. 217.

5. Interview with Vernon Jarrett, September 3, 1998.

6. *Take Me to Chicago The Promised Land*.

7. Henry Steele Commager, ed., *Documents of American History*, 6th ed. (New York: Appleton-Century-Crofts, Inc., 1958), vol. 2, p. 4.

8. Alben Hosley, "Learning How to Be Black," *American Mercury*, vol. XVI, April 1929, p. 424.

9. Benjamin Mays, *Born to Rebel: An Autobiography* (New York: 1971), p. 45.

10. Clifton Daniel, *Chronicle of the 20th Century* (Mount Kisco, N.Y.: Chronicle Publications, Inc., 1987), p. 568.

11. Leon F. Litwack, *Been in the Storm So Long: The Aftermath of Slavery* (New York: Alfred A. Knopf, 1979), p. 531.

12. Richard Wright, *Black Boy: A Record of Childhood and Youth* (New York: 1945), p. 164.

13. Litwack, *Trouble in Mind*, p. 253.

14. Ibid., p. 284.

15. Donald Bogle, *Blacks in American Films and Television: An Illustrated Encyclopedia* (New York: Garland, 1988), p. 19.

16. Interview with Vernon Jarrett, September 3, 1998.

Chapter 4. "Separate but Equal"

1. Leonard Stevens, *Equal! The Case of Integration vs. Jim Crow* (New York: Coward, McCann, and Geohagen, 1976), p. 48.

2. Ibid., p. 49.

3. Geoffrey R. Stone, Louis M. Sedman, Cass R. Sunstein, and Mark V. Tushnet, *Constitutional Law*, 2nd ed. (Boston: Little, Brown, and Company, 1991), p. 489.

4. Stevens, p. 59.

5. Ibid.

6. Bernard Schwartz, *A History of the Supreme Court* (New York: Oxford University, 1993), p. 188.

Chapter 5. Action or Accommodation

1. Columbus Salley, *The Black 100: A Ranking of the Most Influential African-Americans Past and Present* (New York: Carol Publishing, 1993), p. 17.

2. Robert Gardner and Dennis Shortelle, *The Forgotten Players: The Story of Black Baseball in America* (New York: Walker and Company, 1992), p. 10.

3. Jerome B. Agel, ed., "Social Equality Is the Extremest Folly: Booker T. Washington Represents the Negro Race, 1895," *Words That Make America Great* (New York: Random House, 1997), p. 123.

4. Emma Lou Thornbrough, ed., *Booker T. Washington* (Englewood Cliffs, N.J.: Prentice Hall, 1969), p. 14.

5. Booker T. Washington, "The Negro's Life of Slavery," quoted in Thornbrough, p. 30.

6. Thornbrough, p. 17.

7. Ida B. Wells, *Crusade for Justice*, quoted in Leon F. Litwack, *Trouble in Mind: Black Southerners in the Age of Jim Crow* (New York: Alfred A. Knopf, 1998), p. 156.

8. Salley, p. 114.

9. Thornbrough, p. 103.

10. Ibid., p. 105.

11. Arnold Adolff, ed., *Black on Black: Commentaries by Negro Americans* (New York: MacMillan, 1968), p. 38.

Chapter 6. "Come North"

1. Interview with Margaret Burroughs, September 22, 1998.

2. Quoted in James R. Grossman, *Land of Hope: Chicago, Black Southerners, and the Great Migration* (Chicago: University of Chicago, 1989), p. 17.

3. "Additional Letters of Negro Migrants 1916–1919," *Journal of Negro History*, October 1919, quoted in Grossman, p. 3.

4. Nicholas Lemann, *The Promised Land: The Great Black Migration and How It Changed America* (New York: Vintage Books, 1992), p. 47.

5. *Chicago Defender*, January 16, 1915, quoted in Grossman, p. 33.

6. *Take Me to Chicago The Promised Land* (Discovery, British Broadcasting Corporation, 1989).

7. Interview with Margaret Burroughs, September 22, 1998.

8. Richard Wright, *American Negro*, quoted in Grossman, p. 117.

9. Interview with Vernon Jarrett, September 3, 1998.

10. Ibid.

11. Richard Wright, *Black Boy: A Record of Childhood and Youth* (New York: 1945), p. 147.

Chapter 7. The Key to Independence

1. Leonard A. Stevens, *Equal! The Case of Integration vs. Jim Crow* (New York: Coward, McCann, and Geohagen, 1976), p. 63.

2. *The Road to Brown* (California Newsreel, 1989).

3. Stevens, p. 76.

4. *The Road to Brown*.

5. Stevens, p. 101.

6. Geoffrey R. Stone, Louis M. Sedman, Cass R. Sunstein, and Mark V. Tushnet, *Constitutional Law*, 2nd ed. (Boston: Little, Brown, and Company, 1991), p. 504.

7. Robert G. McCloskey, *The American Supreme Court*, 2nd ed. (Chicago: The University of Chicago Press, 1994), pp. 148–149.

8. Clayborne Carson et al., eds., *The Eyes on the Prize Civil Rights Reader* (New York: Viking Penguin, 1991), p. 98.

9. Richard Goldstein, *Mine Eyes Have Seen: A First-Person History of the Events That Shaped America* (New York: Touchstone, 1997), p. 323.

Chapter 8. "If Not Us, Who?"

1. Jo Ann Robinson, *The Montgomery Bus Boycott and the Women Who Started It: The Memoir of Jo Ann Gibson Robinson* (Knoxville: University of Tennessee, 1987), p. xv.

2. Richard Goldstein, *Mine Eyes Have Seen: A First-Person History of the Events That Shaped America* (New York: Touchstone, 1997), p. 321.

3. Mary Hull, *Rosa Parks: Civil Rights Leader* (New York: Chelsea House, 1994), p. 2.

4. Rosa Parks, "The Front of the Bus," *Eyewitness to America: 500 Years of America in the Words of Those Who Saw It Happen*, ed. David Colbert (New York: Pantheon Books, 1997), p. 456.

5. David Halberstam, *The Fifties* (New York: Fawcett Columbine, 1993), p. 556.

6. Robinson, p. 61.

7. Martin Luther King, Jr., *Stride Toward Freedom: The Montgomery Story* (New York: Harper & Bros., 1958), p. 173.

8. Hunter Jones, *They Didn't Put That on the Huntley-Brinkley: A Vagabond Reporter Encounters the New South* (Athens: University of Georgia, 1993), p. 113.

9. David Halberstam, *The Children* (New York: Random House, 1998), p. 93.

10. Jones, p. 118.

11. Casey King and Linda Burnett Osborne, *Oh, Freedom! Kids Talk About the Civil Rights Movement with the People Who Made It Happen* (New York: Alfred A. Knopf, 1997), p. 62.

12. Halberstam, *The Children*, p. 146.

Chapter 9. The Right to Serve, the Right to Vote

1. Statement of policy submitted by Robert P. Patterson, assistant secretary of war, and approved by President Franklin D. Roosevelt, October 9, 1940.

2. Leon F. Litwack, *Trouble in Mind: Black Southerners in the Age of Jim Crow* (New York: Alfred A. Knopf, 1998), p. 224.

3. Martin Luther King, Jr., "A Letter from the Selma, Ala. Jail," quoted in Clayborne Carson et al., eds., *The Eyes on the Prize Civil Rights Reader* (New York: Viking Penguin, 1991), p. 212.

4. David Halberstam, *The Children* (New York: Random House, 1998), p. 504.

5. Ibid., p. 516.

Chapter 10. Violence and Victory

1. Editors of Time-Life Books, *This Fabulous Century 1960–1970* (New York: Time-Life, 1970), p. 147.

2. David Halberstam, *The Fifties* (New York: Fawcett Columbine, 1993), p. 434.

3. Charles Evers and Andrew Szarton, *Have No Fear: The Charles Evers Story* (New York: John Wiley & Sons, Inc., 1997), p. 87.

4. Quoted in John Dittmer, *Local People: The Struggle for Civil Rights in Mississippi* (Urbana, Ill.: University of Illinois, 1994), p. 246.

5. David Halberstam, *The Children* (New York: Random House, 1998), p. 340.

6. Clayborne Carson et al., eds., *The Eyes on the Prize Civil Rights Reader* (New York: Viking Penguin, 1991), pp. 418–419.

7. Jerome B. Agel, ed., "Mississippi and Alabama Will Be Transformed: Martin Luther King, Jr., Has a Dream, 1963," *Words That Make America Great* (New York: Random House, 1997), p. 166.

8. Clifton Daniel, ed., *Chronicle of America* (Famborough, Hampshire, England: J. L. International Publishing, 1989), p. 803.

9. Carson et al., p. 418.

★ FURTHER READING ★

Books

Candaele, Kerry. *Bound for Glory 1910–1930*. New York: Chelsea House, 1997.

Fireside, Harvey. *Plessy v. Ferguson: Separate but Equal?* Springfield, N.J.: Enslow Publishers, Inc., 1997.

——, and Sarah Betsy Fuller. *Brown v. Board of Education: Equal Schooling for All*. Hillside, N.J.: Enslow Publishers, Inc., 1994.

Foner, Eric. *Reconstruction: America's Unfinished Revolution 1863–1877*. New York: Harper & Row, 1988.

Fremon, David K. *The Negro Baseball Leagues*. New York: New Discovery, 1994.

Hauser, Pierre. *Great Ambitions: From the "Separate but Equal" Doctrine to the Birth of the NAACP*. San Diego: Chelsea House, 1995.

Hull, Mary. *Rosa Parks: Civil Rights Leader*. New York: Chelsea House, 1994.

King, Casey, and Linda Bennett Osborne, *Oh, Freedom! Kids Talk About the Civil Rights Movement with the People Who Made It Happen*. New York: Alfred A. Knopf, 1997.

Litwack, Leon F. *Trouble in Mind: Black Southerners in the Age of Jim Crow*. New York: Alfred A. Knopf, 1998.

Internet Addresses

Afro-American Almanac. "The Origin of 'Jim Crow.'" *Afro-American Almanac Historical Documents*. 1996. <http://www.toptags.com/aama/docs/jcrow.htm> (February 23, 2000).

Bowdoin College. "Plessy v. Ferguson, 163 U.S. 537 (1896)." *The Supreme Court Archives*. 1998–1999. <http://www.bowdoin.edu/~sbodurt2/court/index.html> (February 23, 2000).

"'Jim Crow' Laws." *Martin Luther King, Jr., National Historic Site*. January 5, 1998. <http://www.nps.gov/malu/documents/jim_crow_laws.htm> (February 23, 2000).

Library of Congress. "From Jim Crow to Linda Brown: A Retrospective of African-American Experience from 1897 to 1953." *American Memory*. December 1998. <http://lcweb2.loc.gov/ammem/ndlpedu/lesson97/crow/crowhome.html> (February 23, 2000).

National Park Service. *Brown v. Board of Education National Historic Site*. August 6, 1999. <http://www.nps.gov/brvb/> (February 23, 2000).

Tuttle, Kate. "Jim Crow." *Africana.com*. 1999. <http://www.africana.com/tt_026.htm> (February 23, 2000).

★ INDEX ★